THE ONE BREAD

THE ONE BREAD

by MAX THURIAN
Brother of Taizé

translated by Theodore DuBois

SHEED AND WARD : NEW YORK

Contents

Preface   7

PART 1: THE ONE BREAD
The One Bread: Memorial and Invocation   15
The Real Presence   36
Priesthood and Ministry in the Church   45
Intercommunion: Various Conceptions and Observations   89

PART 2: CRISIS OF THE FAITH
The Crisis of Faith   103
Cleansing Secularization   111
The World in the Church   119

5

Demand for Reinterpretation   126

The Permanence of Contemplation   132

Simplifying the Institution   143

Unity among Sister-Churches   153

Conclusion   158

Preface

Today, the Christian is constantly solicited to accept the tension which the church is experiencing between fidelity to the eternal gospel and openness to the modern world. The pages which follow do not pretend to ease this sometimes painful tension. Hopefully, we must continue to experience tension, in order to see the necessary equilibrium between continuity and present relevance emerge from the very history which God makes. This book is rather the reflection on conversations with laymen who are engaged in a search which is sometimes troubled but never deceived by this age of dizziness and passion in a changing church extending itself to new perspectives yet still basing all of its strength on hope nourished by faith and prayer.

Many works are bringing clarity to this difficult debate at the present time. We should reread Dietrich Bonhoeffer, this witness to Jesus Christ among his brethren, as René Marlé so aptly named him. Alan Richardson, in *Religion in Contemporary Debate,* Lesslie Newbigin, in *Honest Religion for Secular Man,* both contribute to this difficult search for a simple and true Christianity for today. Our list would be long if we had to enumerate all of the fraternal theologians who are giving their time and their lives to help Christians in their search, such as Karl Rahner who is always at the avant-garde of the dialogue and Hans Urs von Balthasar who, in *Cordula,* reminds us that we are always both free and crucified in our relationship with the world. Harvey Cox tells us to banish our fear of treason in a secularized world; even though we cannot always follow him, the "secular city" has become the place for a young and living Christianity. Why should the church tremble, since in its poverty it is the body of Christ?

Therefore, the pages that follow seek to constitute a dialogue with Christians who want to be both faithful to the tradition of the gospel and relevant in the contemporary world. In recalling this frank faithfulness and healthy modernity, I think now as I often do of Father Henri de Lubac; I have just read "Teilhard and Our Times," the second part of his last work *The Feminine Eternal.* Behind the thought of another, Henri de Lubac hides and humbly reveals this theology of a personal God, of Christ and of the church, which makes him a master in evangelical tradition and a sure guide to true and free obedience.

To the degree that Christians feel profoundly united in the search for a solution to today's crisis of faith, they find it more and more difficult to be separated into different churches and particularly to be hindered from communicating together in the same Eucharist.

Recent ecumenical progress, which has been almost miraculous, has sparked a real revolution as it has led Christians to live in authentic fidelity to the gospel. Once one has embarked on this path, however, an irresistible pressure begins to build up and the visible unity so avidly sought begins to appear far too distant. It is then that the desire is born to skip the intervening stages, since the goal must be reached by whatever means.

Now is perhaps the time to recall an essential requirement of ecumenism: respect for conscience. Sometimes the legitimate ardor which spurs them on leads Christians to unconsciously demand from each other abdications of conscience whose price, unfortunately, seems less and less as the achievement of unity seems nearer at hand. It is, nevertheless, quite clear that authentic unity can only be born of loyalty and fidelity on both sides. Protestants hailed the accomplishment of the Council when, under the leadership of the Secretariat for Unity, it replaced the idea of "the great return" with "spiritual emulation" as the keynote of Christian reconciliation. They must not now desire to see Christian unity rapidly achieved at the price of asking their catholic and orthodox brothers to minimize ecclesial obedience.

Intercommunion, which is so avidly desired by many Christians, requires a basic common faith, firm mutual commitment and a true communal life. The necessary content for eucharistic intercommunion is a real intercommunion in faith and life, theology and commitment. I would like to underline one cardinal point. Granting the agreement of the churches concerned, eucharistic intercommunion could only have its full significance if the "protestants" who participated in it committed themselves to absorb into their own faith a profound understanding of what ministerial ordination and episcopal structure mean for a "catholic." On the other hand, this same experience would demand "protestant" pastorate. We are certainly on our way, but have we arrived at this degree of vital commitment, which is the necessary condition for any common

Eucharist—once again taking for granted the agreement of the churches?

The report on intercommunion of the archepiscopal commission of the Anglican Church has just appeared and in chapter twelve which concerns concelebration, two important paragraphs are addressed to "joint celebration" (paras. 200-201). The position of the Anglican Church is specifically its own, of course, but it is interesting to examine the point of view expressed here because it is new for an episcopal church which believes in the value of historical apostolic succession:

> Where the possibility of reciprocal intercommunion is already accepted, joint celebration is feasible. In this two or more congregations come together to celebrate one eucharist using the same rite and the same elements with the ministers of the different communions acting together on behalf of all the assembled people of God and together communicating the joint congregation. This should be seen as a way of expressing reciprocal intercommunion, not as a way of making it acceptable by cloaking scruples about the status of the ministries involved. It may commend itself as an appropriate and honest way of celebrating together in a situation where the one loaf and the common cup correspond to a genuine spiritual reality, but where there is no single authorised ministry but mutual recognition of differing ministries and mutual acceptance of communicants.
>
> The form of such joint celebration need not differ from the concelebration appropriate to conditions of full communion or organic union. Such a celebration presupposes the presence or permission of the bishop, an invitation to one minister to act as president or chief celebrant (appropriately the minister of the host church) and agreement on a common rite (whether of one of the participating congregations or of a "neutral" kind such as Taizé or South India or some experimental liturgy). Some relaxation of the legal restrictions on

the ministers in this last regard would of course be necessary. The practical details (providing scruples about alcoholic wine raise no objection) would be no more difficult, and need be no more uniform, than in the case of concelebration proper. Participation, aloud or in silence, of all the ministers in the eucharistic prayer would be presupposed: otherwise the words and actions can be shared or divided between all the concelebrating members of the people of God, ordained and lay, according to the part in the liturgy appropriate to each.

This extremely interesting move toward further openness on the part of the Anglican Church once more testifies to its privileged position in terms of visible Christian unity. Christians, especially the young, will certainly press more and more strongly for a realization of eucharistic unity. It must be possible, and it certainly is preferable that the authorities of the various churches anticipate this pressure, which might otherwise prove harmful for the faith. The Eucharist is a sacrament of the church, and only the church can organize its celebration. But it is precisely love for Christ's church that leads these Christians to want the church to march at the head of the movement toward unity rather than be obliged someday to have to make do with an unwelcome revolution.

Part 1
THE ONE BREAD

The fact that there is only one loaf means that, though there are many of us, we form a single body because we all have a share in this one loaf (1 Cor. 10:17).

Dialogue should be undertaken concerning the true meaning of the Lord's Supper, the other sacraments, and the Church's worship and ministry (The Decree on Ecumenism of the Second Vatican Council, No. 22).

familiar with the Jewish religion. The memorial evoked in the minds of the people a liturgical reality and an idea of profound spiritual contact with the Lord. In this way, when the Roman centurion, Cornelius, had the vision described to us in the Acts of the Apostles (10:1 ff.), the Angel of God told him, "Your offering of prayers and alms has ascended as a memorial before God" (Acts 10:4). When he describes his vision to Peter, Cornelius uses the liturgical term, memorial, explicitly as a recalling of his prayers and his charity before God. "Three days ago I was praying in my house at the ninth hour, when I suddenly saw a man in front of me in shining robes. He said, 'Cornelius, your prayer has been heard and your alms have been accepted as a sacrifice in the sight of God'" (Acts 10:30-31).

The idea according to which prayers and charity, like sacrifices, are presented before God "as a memorial" is part of the liturgical theology of Judaism. We find it as a basic premise in both the Old and the New Testaments, and the word which designates it is therefore equivalent to the one Christ pronounced when he said, "Do this as a memorial of me."

In his last book, *Eucharistie,* Father Louis Bouyer analyses the benedictions of the Jewish liturgy and confirms irrefutably the sacrificial meaning of the anamnesis, the eucharistic memorial.

In the third benediction of the liturgy of meals, it is very interesting to note that ancient rabbinic tradition prescribes a variant for feast days. We can imagine Christ saying this prayer during the meal in which he instituted the Eucharist, and in this way giving all of its meaning to the word "memorial," "zikkaron" in Hebrew, "anamnesis" in Greek:

> Our God and the God of our fathers! May the memorial of ourselves and of our fathers, the memorial of Jerusalem, your city, the memorial of the Messiah, the son of David, your

servant, and the memorial of your people, of all the house of Israel, rise up and come, may it arrive, be seen, accepted, heard, recalled and mentioned before you, for deliverance, good, forgiveness, compassion and mercy, on this day of (the name of the feast day is pronounced). Remember us, Lord, our God, to do us good and visit us because of it and save us for sake of it, renewing us by a word of salvation and mercy: spare us, forgive us and show us your mercy, for you are a God and a King of forgiveness and mercy.

During the holy supper, which is situated in the liturgical atmosphere of the paschal meal and uses its themes, the church, according to the command of its Lord, performs an act "as the memorial of Christ": it offers thanksgiving for the unique and perfect deliverance which was accomplished in the passion and the resurrection; it also offers thanksgiving for the fact that this deliverance is actualized by the sacrament; and finally, it prays God that this salvation be applied to each man by Christ's coming into him, and that the Messiah will return soon to accomplish with splendor in the Kingdom for the whole universe what he has already accomplished in a hidden way in it, by the abasement of his Incarnation. It is in this perspective that we must understand the eucharistic acclamation which ends St. Paul's first epistle to the Corinthians, "Maranatha" (16:22), which can be translated as, "The Lord is coming," or, "Lord, come!" The ambiguity of this Aramaic acclamation which passed into primitive Christian liturgical language summarizes the entire meaning of the Eucharist as that of the paschal meal, a thanksgiving for a given fact, past and present: the Lord is coming, and ardent supplication for Christ's return: Lord, come! Like the paschal meal, the holy supper follows the movement which goes from faith in a deliverance that is accomplished and operative in the sacrament, to a prayer that the Lord come into every man and thus hasten the last day. Need we emphasize that all the difference between these two analogous movements is that the paschal meal sets out from a typical deliverance to announce and implore another definitive deliverance to come, whereas the holy supper sets out from the definitive deliverance hidden in Christ to proclaim and implore the glorious manifestation of this same and unique liberation. The deliverance of the people of Israel, their journey out of Egypt, which was the foundation of their existence as the People of God, could be shared in the sacrament of the paschal meal, but it could also be annihilated by sin; it therefore supposed a true, total and definitive liberation by the Messiah which was to come on the day of the Passover. The salvation of the church, the Body of Christ, can be given to its members in the sacrament of the Eucharist, but it can never be lost or compromised by the sin of individuals; it does not suppose a second, salvific intervention by God, but only a manifestation, in the glory of the Kingdom, of a reality hidden in the mystery of the church.

During the time between the objective redemption, effected by the passion and resurrection of Christ and his glorious return, the Lord remembers his covenant, and he actualizes, dispenses, distributes and individualizes the salvation accomplished once for all. This remembrance of the covenant is frequently mentioned in the Old Testament; the Jewish liturgy for the new year contains prayers, the "zikronot," which are striking in this sense. They consist of biblical passages where God is spoken of as recalling the promises of his covenant in the past and in the future. The concluding prayer ends with, "May you be praised, Lord, for recalling the covenant." In the holy supper, we have the same certitude of the faithfulness of him who said, "This is my body . . . This cup is the new covenant in my blood." God is faithful and forever recalls the New Covenant concluded forever in his Son with the church, the Body of

Christ. The Eucharist implies this certitude of God's faithful remembrance; it is thanksgiving for this faithfulness and its certainty, but it is also confident intercession that God's remembrance be applied to the sinners we all are. Moses, interceding for Israel, said to his Lord: "Remember Abraham, Isaac and Jacob, your servants to whom by your own self you swore and made this promise: 'I will make your offspring as many as the stars of heaven, and all this land which I promised I will give to your descendants, and it shall be their heritage for ever'" (Ex. 32:13). The covenant with the patriarchs is irrevocable; and yet Moses intercedes with the Lord that he remember it today for sinners, and that he apply to an apostate Israel, to an Israel which has just prostrated itself before the Golden Calf, the promises he made to Abraham, Isaac, and Jacob: "Remember Abraham . . ." In the Eucharist, the church makes the same intercession, presenting the crucified Christ to God so that the Father will remember in our favor the New Covenant concluded on the cross, both now and personally for each sinner. The church might well say: "Remember Christ crucified, because it is in him alone that everything has been accomplished for the salvation of sinners; remember him who has said, 'Do this as a memorial of me,' and let us apply today the blessings which his death won for us."

The command to perform the eucharistic act can be explained by the words which have now become so rich in meaning: ". . . as a memorial of me, in memory of me, to remember me . . ." This memorial is not a merely subjective remembrance; it is a liturgical act. It is not merely a liturgical act which makes the Lord present; it is a liturgical act which recalls before the Father the memorial of the unique sacrifice of the Son who makes it present in his memorial, in the presentation of his sacrifice before the Father and in his intercession as heavenly High Priest. The eucharistic memorial is a remembrance to us, to the Father through us and to the Father by the Son for us. Thus, the eucharistic memorial is a proclamation to the church, a thanksgiving and an intercession on the part of the church, a thanksgiving and an intercession on the part of Christ for the church.

In celebrating the Eucharist, the church places on the altar the signs of Christ's sacrifice, the bread and wine, his Body and Blood, as Israel placed the loaves of proposition on the golden table as a memorial before God. The church, in proclaiming the sacrifice of Christ, accomplishes on the altar the pro-position of the Son's sacrifice before the Father, in thanksgiving and in intercession, in praise and in supplication. In this way, the church participates in this act of pro-position of the cross, in the pro-position of the Lamb as the immolated victim on the heavenly altar and in the pro-position which the Son makes of his sacrifice before the Father, in thanksgiving and intercession.

In accomplishing this "proposition" of the sacrifice of the cross, in union with that of the Son before the Father, the church performs the memorial of Christ's entire redemptive work; the church offers thanksgiving for everything he has done for us and intercedes before the Father that he pour down on men the blessings which the Son acquired by means of all that he accomplished. This thanksgiving and intercession of the memorial is constituted by the act itself of celebrating the Eucharist and not merely by the prayers which state it explicitly. When we repeat the acts which Christ performed at the holy supper, we accomplish the memorial of thanksgiving and intercession. The thanksgiving and intercession are not expressed only by words, but by the total act of the celebration: Christ's acts with Christ's signs, the bread and wine placed on the altar, "the bread that we break and the blessing-cup that we bless" (I Cor. 10:16).

The bread that is broken, the wine that is poured out, the body and the blood presented separately, the mention of the Covenant in blood, all are signs of the sacrifice on the cross and of the intercession in heaven of Christ, the High Priest of the church. This recalling of the cult of the Old Covenant, the sacrifice for sin and the aspersion with blood in the Holy of Holies, truly makes the Eucharist the sacrament of the sacrifice for sin on the cross and of the Son's intercession in the heavenly sanctuary. By means of the Eucharist, the sacrifice for sin on the cross and the Son's intercession in heaven are made present to the church. The church enters into communion with Christ, the High Priest, in his heavenly intercession which effects the sacrifice of the Covenant and the sacrifice for sin accomplished on the cross. With him and in him, the church presents to the Father this sacrifice, the broken bread and the poured out wine, the immolated body and the spilled blood, and in this way intercedes for the forgiveness of sins and for the needs of all the people and at the same time offers thanksgiving for all the wonders accomplished.

This body handed over and this blood poured out were given and poured out in sacrifice on the cross "for many." In the Eucharist, this same body and this same blood, sacrament of the presence of the sacrifice of the cross, are presented to the Father in an act of thanksgiving and intercession, in the Son's communion of heavenly praise and intercession in the midst of the saints. "For you" or "for many" still signify today that the bread broken and given, the wine poured out, the body and blood of the Son presented to the Father, are the most efficacious intercession the church can make for the faithful and for all men; the church presents to the Father, in intercession, the signs or the sacrament of the gift which the Son offered to the

Father on the cross for us and for all men. And this sacrament of the gift offered by the Son to the Father for us is at the same time the sacrament of the gift bestowed by God on all the faithful and on all men. The church receives this gift in communion. However, we must not separate the memorial from the communion, the sacrament of the Son's sacrifice offered to the Father from the sacrament of Christ's presence given to the church. The eucharistic celebration is an indivisible whole: the sacrament of sacrifice to the Father and the sacrament of presence to the church constitute one and the same sacrament in the perspective of Christ's prayer according to St. John: "Father, may they be one in us, as you are in me and I am in you, so that the world may believe it was you who sent me" (Jn. 17:21). The gift of union with the Father and the Son is the special gift of the Eucharist, the gift of Christ's Body which nourishes Christ's ecclesial Body. This gift of union with God is bound up with the unity of the Father and the Son in the Incarnation and sacrifice, and the fruit of this union is the evangelization of the world. In the Eucharist, the sacrament of the sacrifice and the sacrament of the presence are one: Christ is present to his church in the signs of his sacrifice to the Father, and the church also presents the memorial of his sacrifice when it receives the crucified Lord in communion. Christ's words at the holy supper were preceded by an invitation to communion. Before he presented his body and his blood separately, the signs of the sacrifice, the Lord said: "Take and eat . . . Drink all of you . . ." Whatever the variations in these words transmitted by the gospels, they indicate an indissoluble relationship between the communion and the memorial of the sacrifice. Therefore, the communion should always be part of the eucharistic celebration because it is in the communion, as in the celebration which includes communion, that we perform the memorial of the sacrifice of the cross, unite ourselves to

Christ's heavenly intercession and commune with his real presence, with his body and blood offered for us to the Father.

In this way, the church, by means of the Eucharist, accomplishes Christ's memorial, presents his sacrifice to the Father, participates in his heavenly intercession and "proclaims the death of the Lord until he comes," in the act of thanksgiving of the entire eucharistic prayer which recalls the work of the redemption. In the breaking of the bread, the body of Christ is handed over for us; in the chalice of poured out wine, the blood of Christ and of the New Covenant is poured out for us for the remission of sins. We present Christ's body and blood on the altar, separate as they were in the immolation on the cross, by taking, eating and drinking the eucharistic species in communion. In one single eucharistic act which includes the word of God (readings), praise (psalms and responses), prayer (orations and intercession), the church's offering (the offertory), thanksgiving (eucharistic prayer) and communion (from the Lord's Prayer to the blessing), the liturgy presents the sacrifice of the cross and unites us to the heavenly intercession until the return of the Lord. Thus, the church accomplishes the memorial of the Lord in a liturgical act of perfect unity, obeys his command, "Do this as a memorial of me," and proclaims the death of the Lord until he returns.

Because they had lost a living contact with the Bible and its doctrine regarding Christ's eucharistic memorial, certain theologians of the Middle Ages insisted far too much on the sacrificial aspect of the Mass. As a result, the Mass began to appear to be a repetition of Christ's unique sacrifice. Sixteenth century Protestants felt that the doctrine of the sacrifice of the Mass contradicted the doctrine of the uniqueness of the sacrifice of the cross for the forgiveness of sins. Therefore, they insisted almost exclusively on the character of meal, communion and gift in the holy supper.

The process of division prevented Catholic and Protestant theologians from understanding each other and from returning to unity after their mutual criticisms. In the seventeenth century, Reformed theologians made a considerable attempt to again attain the doctrine that the Eucharist is the sacrificial memorial of the cross. One of these was Pierre du Moulin who, in 1635, when asked in what sense the holy supper could be called a sacrifice, replied:

> 1) Because this Sacrament was instituted to announce the Lord's death until he returns. The Holy Supper can be called a sacrifice because it represents the sacrifice of the Lord's death; and signs and representations usually take the name of what they signify.
>
> 2) It is possible to say that in the Holy Supper we offer Jesus Christ to God, inasmuch as we pray God that he accept for us the sacrifice of his death.
>
> 3) The Holy Supper is a sacrifice of Eucharist, that is, of thanksgiving for God's blessings, and especially for the blessing which is our redemption by Jesus Christ . . . (*The Shield of Faith*).

Catholic and Protestant theologians might be able to agree on such formulas, but centuries of separation have widened the distance between them. Catholics insisted more and more on the sacrificial aspect of the Mass, forgetting its character as a meal and even neglecting the intimate connection between celebration of the Mass and communion of the faithful. Protestants forgot the eucharistic memorial's character as a sacrifice of praise and prayer and saw no more in it than a symbolic meal uniting them spiritually to the crucified Christ.

It was not until the biblical and liturgical renewals of recent years that both parties rediscovered these complementary aspects of the Eucharist. There was renewed awareness on the part of Protestants of the Eucharist as a sacrifice of thanksgiving for God's wonderful deeds in salvation history and of intercession that he renew these wonders for all men today. Catholics, for their part, came to recognize the Eucharist as the meal in which Christ offers himself as food and in which we are invited to participate in communion.

A wide moat was dug, but today bridges are being built across it. We will cite two texts here which give evidence that an ecumenical convergence exists with regard to the Eucharist as the sacrificial memorial of the Lord really present, a convergence which is surely going to develop all the way to the day when it will bring us to unity of faith.

The first text is from the ecumenical conference which took place in Montreal in 1963. At this conference, theologians representing Protestantism, Anglicanism, and Orthodoxy agreed on the following points:

Despite many disagreements regarding Holy Communion and despite the desire of many for a fuller statement, we are drawn at least to agree that the Lord's Supper, a gift of God to his Church, is a sacrament of the presence of the crucified and glorified Christ until he come, and a means whereby the sacrifice of the cross, which we proclaim, is operative within the Church. In the Lord's Supper the members of the body of Christ are sustained in their unity with their Head and Saviour who offered himself on the cross; by him, with him and in him who is our great High Priest and Intercessor we offer to the Father, in the power of the Holy Spirit, our praise, thanksgiving and intercession. With contrite hearts we offer ourselves as a living and holy sacrifice, a sacrifice which must be expressed in the whole of our daily lives. Thus united to our Lord and to the Church triumphant, and in fellowship with the whole Church on earth, we are renewed in the covenant sealed by the blood of Christ. In the supper we also anticipate the marriage-supper of the Lamb in the Kingdom of God.[1]

The second text is the introduction to the chapter on the Eucharist in the Constitution on the Liturgy from Vatican II:

At the Last Supper, on the night when He was betrayed, our Savior instituted the Eucharistic Sacrifice of His Body and Blood. He did this in order to perpetuate the sacrifice of the Cross throughout the centuries until He should come again, and so to entrust to His beloved spouse, the Church, a memorial of His death and resurrection: a sacrament of love, a sign of unity, a bond of charity, a paschal banquet in which Christ is consumed, the mind is filled with grace, and a pledge of future glory is given to us.

The Church, therefore, earnestly desires that Christ's faithful, when present at this mystery of faith, should not be there as strangers or silent spectators. On the contrary, through a proper appreciation of the rites and prayers they should participate knowingly, devoutly, and actively. They should be instructed by God's word and be refreshed at the table of the Lord's body; they should give thanks to God; by offering the Immaculate Victim, not only through the hands of the priest, but also with him, they should learn to offer themselves too. Through Christ the Mediator, they should be drawn day by day into ever closer union with God and with each other, so that finally God may be all in all.

[1] The Fourth World Conference on Faith and Order, Montreal, 1963. Edited by P. C. Rodger and Lukas Vischer (New York, Association Press, 1964), p. 73.

THE INVOCATION OF THE SPIRIT

All the life, word and action of the Son of God in his Incarnation is accomplished in the power of the Holy Spirit. It is the Holy Spirit who conceived Christ in Mary on the day of the Incarnation, who bestowed the messianic unction on Christ at his baptism in the Jordan, who led him into the desert to be tempted, and who filled him with his power for his ministry (cf. Lk. 1:35; 3:22; 4:1,14, 18-19, etc.). During the time of the Incarnation, the Holy Spirit's role is to manifest Christ's continual dependence on the Father: he does nothing which the Father does not tell him to do, and what he does is done in the power of the Spirit. The mention of the Spirit's work in the life of Christ underlines the fact that the Son's Incarnation does not exhaust God's work, and that it remains an act willed by the Father and sustained by the Holy Spirit. The Spirit's role in the Son's terrestrial life underlines the trinitarian action at the time of the Incarnation and prohibits any christomonism in theological thought. Christ is the fullness of God only because he is the Son sent from the Father, and because he lives, speaks and acts in the power of the Spirit.

When the risen Christ gives the apostles their mission, he breathes on them, signifying the gift of the Spirit, and he commands them to baptize in the name of the Father and of the Son and of the Holy Spirit (Jn. 20:22-23; Mt. 28:19). On the day of Pentecost, the apostles receive the fullness of the Holy Spirit according to Christ's promise; the Spirit will be for them: "another Advocate to be with them for ever, that Spirit of truth who will lead them to the complete truth" (Jn. 14:16; 16:13). Just as the Son in his Incarnation was not alone the fullness of God, neither will the Spirit exhaust God's action after Pentecost. He will not speak of himself, he will speak of everything that he will hear, he will glorify Christ, he will take from what belongs to Christ and share it with the apostles, he will teach them everything and recall to them everything that Christ said to them (Jn. 16:13-14; 14:26). Therefore, the Father will send the Holy Spirit in the Son's name; everything that belongs to the Father belongs to the Son; and this is why the Spirit will obtain from the Son what he gives to the apostles and to the church (Jn. 14:26; 16:15). Therefore, the Holy Spirit will manifest himself to the apostles as a person, another Advocate, who remains at their side and whom they can invoke as their counselor, consoler and defender. He remains with them, and he is even in them (Jn. 14:17). It is the Holy Spirit, sent by the Father and witness to the Son, who clothes the apostles with his power in the exercise of their mission and their ministry.

In the light of the mysteries of the Ascension and Pentecost, we can understand the necessity and the meaning of the epiclesis in the Eucharist, i.e. the invocation of the Holy Spirit on the Eucharist. The Ascension sets in relief Christ's epicletic intercession as Priest and King; Pentecost manifests God's response to this epiclesis.

In the epistle to the Hebrews, the mystery of the Ascension is expressed by referring to the acts in the Jewish liturgy of Expiations:

> But now Christ has come, as the high priest of all the blessings which were to come. He has passed through the greater, the more perfect tent, which is better than the one made by men's hands because it is not of this created order; and he has entered the sanctuary once and for all, taking with him not the blood of goats and bull calves, but his own blood, having won an eternal redemption for us. The blood of goats and bulls and the ashes of a heifer are sprinkled on those who have incurred defilement and they restore the holiness of their outward lives; how much more effectively the blood of Christ, who offered himself as the perfect sacrifice to God through the

eternal Spirit, can purify our inner self from dead actions so that we do our service to the living God (Heb. 9:11-14).

On the Day of Expiations, the high priest entered beyond the veil of the sanctuary, bearing the blood of sacrifice for sin, with which he performed the rite of expiation on the throne of mercy "for the uncleanness of the sons of Israel, for their transgressions and for all their sins" (Lev. 16:16). The rite of expiation for the people was performed in two stages: first, the sacrifice for sin on the altar, then the aspersion with blood in the sanctuary, beyond the veil, on the throne of mercy. The author of the epistle to the Hebrews saw in this the symbol of the two stages in Christ's expiation: first, the sacrifice for sin on the altar of the cross, then entrance into the heavenly sanctuary with the blood of the sacrifice as his perpetual intercession. We find here the twofold aspect of the one and unique sacrifice of Christ for the one and unique forgiveness of sins, historical and perpetual, once and for all and unceasingly. We know that the Eucharist's sacrificial character for the forgiveness of sins is connected with this entrance of Christ, the High Priest, into the sanctuary of heaven, beyond the veil, bearing the blood of his sacrifice as a perpetual intercession. The blood of the holy supper is this blood which Christ bore from the cross to the heavenly sanctuary, the symbol of his perpetual intercession for the forgiveness of sins.

The sign of Christ's blood therefore represents the heavenly intercession of the crucified Christ who, by his Ascension, has entered beyond the veil in the heavenly sanctuary like the high priest on the Day of Expiations. He lives forever to intercede in our favor. In a way, he presents to the Father the stigmata of his passion and thus accomplishes the memorial of his unique sacrifice.

According to Christ's promise, "I shall ask the Father, and

he will give you another Advocate to be with you for ever, the Spirit of truth," we can say that the fundamental object of the Son's priestly intercession after the ascension is the gift of the Holy Spirit. Christ, the High Priest, penetrating to the heavenly sanctuary presents the blood of sacrifice, the stigmata of his passion, and accomplishes the memorial of his sacrifice which becomes a living intercession before the Father so that he will send the Spirit on the church. The Son's memorial before the Father is an epiclesis of the Spirit. We see here how anamnesis and epiclesis, memorial of Christ and invocation of the Spirit, are closely linked in the mystery of the Ascension which is the mystery of the Son's intercession before the Father, founded on the memorial of the cross, for the gift of the Spirit to the church. Just as the anamnesis of the Son before the Father becomes an epiclesis of the Spirit, the eucharistic anamnesis becomes a eucharistic epiclesis. Anamnesis and epiclesis are two necessary aspects of the Eucharist. The memorial of the cross in the Eucharist becomes epicletic supplication that the Father give the Holy Spirit in answer to the Son's sacrifice, sacramentally commemorated and presented before him as an ardent intercession.

The Father answered the Son's epicletic intercession when he gave the Holy Spirit to the apostles and the church. Pentecost is the answer to the epiclesis of Christ as Priest and King. As Priest, he performs the memorial of his sacrifice before the Father, his epicletic intercession, whose object is the gift of the Spirit to the church. As King, he becomes, like the Old Testament king, the channel of God's blessings on the people; his epiclesis is answered and the Father sends the Holy Spirit in his name (Jn. 14:26).

This anamnesis-epiclesis of Christ as Priest and King in the mystery of the Ascension and Pentecost gives a clear meaning to the eucharistic anamnesis and epiclesis. The anamnesis is the memorial of the mysteries of Christ, before the church and before God simultaneously, as a presentation for the church and as presentation before God. As propitiation of the mysteries of Christ and especially of the sacrifice of the cross, before the Father, the Eucharist is a thanksgiving for all the blessings which the Son has obtained for the church and an intercession that these blessings be renewed unceasingly. The special blessing asked for is the gift of the Holy Spirit; the fundamental intercession constituted by the anamnesis is the epiclesis of the Spirit. It is this movement from anamnesis to epiclesis, from the priestly intercession of the Ascension to the royal gift of Pentecost, that all liturgies have wanted to express.

We find this movement in the Roman Canon, even if it does not state the name of the Holy Spirit explicitly—a regrettable lacuna. The anamnesis ends with the mention of "the ascension into the glory of heaven," indicating the Eucharist's sacrificial movement; and the anaphora evokes the heavenly memorial on the "altar of glory" and asks that the church may be "filled with grace and blessings." The oriental liturgies are more explicit regarding this movement from the anamnesis of the Son to the epiclesis of the Spirit. But, because of the polemic between the Orient and the Occident, the movement and the dogmatic significance of the eucharistic prayer of anamnesis-epiclesis have become obscure. In the Orient, the anamnesis runs the danger of becoming a simple, historical recital of facts preparatory to to the great consecratory moment of the epiclesis. The Occident puts all the emphasis on the consecratory anamnesis, especially on the words of institution; and it runs the danger of minimizing what remains of the epiclesis by making it a prayer of preparation for communion. We must return to the primitive equilibrium.

The anamnesis of the mysteries of the Son by the church becomes the epiclesis of the gifts of the Spirit on the church.

We should not inquire regarding what is the precise moment of consecration; the entire anaphora is consecratory. The epiclesis after and in the movement of the anamnesis should not take on a consecratory character which would detract from the value of the words of institution; and the words of institution should not appear as a culminating point which would detract from the value of all the rest of the anamnesis and epiclesis. The epiclesis after and in the movement of the anamnesis is essentially an invocation founded on the memorial of Christ. It is the Eucharist's Pentecost, in answer to the priestly intercession of the glorious Christ of the Ascension, an intercession expressed by the anamnesis of the mysteries of Christ and especially by the memorial of his sacrifice. Thus, the Eucharist manifests the unity that exists between the Ascension and Pentecost—the unity between the Son's heavenly intercession in the eternal Spirit before the Father by the anamnesis of his sacrifice, and the Father's gift of the Holy Spirit in the name of the Son to the church in the answer of epiclesis.

However, a problem remains. Isn't there also an epiclesis of the Holy Spirit on the bread and wine of the Eucharist? We have seen that, placed after the anamnesis, this epiclesis confuses the movement of the anaphora and runs the danger of detracting from the words of institution by giving them a purely historical meaning. Since the time of Pentecost, it is the Holy Spirit who is always the first actor in the acts of the church with regard to temporal succession. The Spirit of Truth leads us in complete truth. To be sure, he does not speak about himself, but he says everything which he hears from the Father and the Son. He glorifies the Son: he obtains the goods of the Father and the Son and shares them with us. This is St. John's pneumatological doctrine (Jn. 16:13-15). In the Eucharist, therefore, the Holy Spirit is the first one to act; he obtains the Son's words, "This is my body . . . this is my blood," for us, and he shares their blessings with us. Without the action of the Holy Spirit, what Christ spoke would remain only words; they would act neither on the bread and wine nor on the church. The Holy Spirit makes the entire mystery of Christ live for us; he makes the anamnesis a real presentation, in the church, of the unique sacrifice of the cross and an efficacious memorial, before the Father, of this perfect intercession. We must, therefore, have an epiclesis which expresses this action of the Spirit on the bread and wine, on the words of Christ and on the entire memorial in the Eucharist. It is in the power of the Holy Spirit, invoked by the epiclesis, that the church presents to the Father the memorial of the Son and that it can repeat efficaciously the words of institution: "This is my body . . . this is my blood."

This necessary union between the Spirit and the Son in the eucharistic action and this pre-action of the Spirit on the words of Christ and on the anamnesis should be expressed in the liturgy by an epiclesis closely bound to the words of institution but preceding them. It is possible to discern the development of the history of salvation in a development similar to the eucharistic prayer.

Preface:	thanksgiving for *the creation and the plan of God,* ending with the song of all creatures in Isaiah's prophetic Sanctus.
Epiclesis I:	invocation of the Holy Spirit on the creatures of bread and wine, recalling the coming of the Spirit on Mary at *the Incarnation,* to make manifest the body and blood of Christ.
Institution:	the words by which Christ instituted *the Eucharist* on the eve of his passion.
Anamnesis:	memorial of the mysteries of Christ and especially *the passion, the resurrection, and the ascension;*

sacrificial prayer united to Christ's *heavenly intercession*.

Epiclesis II: invocation of the Holy Spirit on the church, recalling and continuing *Pentecost*.

Conclusion: final doxology, recalling the eternal glory of God the Trinity for ever in *the Kingdom*.

The Real Presence

The primitive church understood Christ's words, "This is my body, this is my blood," in a way that was very simple and both realistic and sacramental: realistic, because Christ spoke truly, and he really is present in the Eucharist; sacramental, because his presence is not carnal like ours. In the Eucharist, the glorious Christ is present to the church in his entire person, but in a sacramental way, a way that is a mystery. For the Fathers of the church, the bread and wine become the body and blood of Christ according to the mystery of God, who takes ordinary bread and wine and makes of them Christ's body and blood, the sacramental signs of his real presence. From a biblical perspective, we can summarize faith in Christ's real presence in the Eucharist.

Christ's body and blood, all of his humanity and divinity, are really present in the Eucharist. This real presence of his body and blood is the presence of Christ crucified and glorious, here and now, under concrete signs. The meaning of every corporal presence is that a person is concretely present, and that he can enter into concrete communication. By the real presence of Christ's body and blood, the church is certain that its Lord is there in its midst concretely and that it receives him under a concrete figure.

The figure of bread and wine is the sign that Christ is our nourishment; this sign of the bread and wine is for us the vehicle of the real presence of Christ's body and blood. This real, corporal presence should be contemplated and received in the liturgical act where Christ acts with us and for us and where he gives himself to us in communion.

Communion with the body and blood of Christ is at the same time a communion of each person with the ecclesial body. United in the same offering which the church makes in Christ, the faithful are bound together indissolubly when they receive the body of Christ in communion.

The church makes the Eucharist, and the Eucharist makes the church. The Eucharist unites and solders the members of Christ's body together. United in the eucharistic and ecclesial body of Christ, the baptized are welded together in unity and can only look toward deepening, prolonging and totally accomplishing their unity. The Eucharist, the sacrament of unity, is the sacrament of the charity which it maintains and deepens. In the life of a local community, the Eucharist is the special bond in which the church constructs itself and deepens itself in charity. The church that frequently celebrates the Eucharist sees Christ, by means of the Eucharist, develop its charity and unity, and it sees him make his word and life efficacious in the world.

This real presence of Christ in the bread and wine, his body and blood, is a mystery which the church can never sound to its very depths. The church can only present it as an indisputable fact and defend faith in the real presence by protecting it against every explanation which minimizes or exaggerates it, against all spiritualism and all carnal magic. St. Irenaeus of Lyons was able to express the mystery of the real presence with this remarkable formula:

> For as the bread, which is produced from the earth, when it receives the invocation of God, is no longer common bread, but the Eucharist, consisting of two realities, earthly and heavenly; so also our bodies, when they receive the Eucharist, are no longer corruptible, having the hope of the resurrection to eternity . . . (*Adversus Haereses* IV, 18, 5).[2]

Luther affirmed with equal force that the bread and wine are Christ's body and blood, but he rejected the concept of transubstantiation, which he looked upon merely as an attempt at explanation: "The sacrament of the altar is the true body and blood of our Lord Jesus Christ, under the bread and wine, so that we Christians might eat and drink, the institution of Christ himself" (*The Little Catechism, VI*).

Calvin also believes in the real presence connected with the sign of the bread. He writes:

> It is a spiritual mystery which cannot be seen by the eye nor be comprehended by human understanding. Therefore, it is represented for us by means of visible signs, according to the need of our weakness; nevertheless, it is not a naked figure, but one joined to its truth and substance. With good reason

[2] *The Anti-Nicene Fathers,* 1 : *The Apostolic Fathers with Justin Martyr and Irenaeus,* edited by A. Roberts and J. Donaldson (Grand Rapids, Mich., Eerdmans, 1962).

then, the bread is called body, because it not only represents, but also presents it. (*Short Treatise on the Holy Supper*).

The Council of Trent speaks of the real presence as a "change" according to which the bread and wine becomes Christ's body and blood; "this change the holy Catholic Church fittingly and properly names transubstantiation."[3] Thus, transubstantiation indicates primarily the reality of Christ's presence, in other words, that he is "truly, really and substantially contained" in the Eucharist.

We can notice the essential agreement that exists between these three positions: Christ is really present in the Eucharist. However, they diverge in their concepts of the mode, the "how," of this real presence. We can designate these three concepts by means of three key-words: transubstantiation (for the Council of Trent), consubstantiation (for Luther) and concomitance (for Calvin).

According to the doctrine of transubstantiation, the substance of the bread and wine, that is, "that which makes the bread and wine what they are as earthly food," the profound being of the bread and wine, is changed and becomes a new being, the body and blood of Christ. There is a substantial change, a change of substance.

According to the doctrine of consubstantiation, the substance, the profound being of the bread and wine, subsists; but it is closely united to the substance, to the profound being, of Christ's body and blood just as the metal and fire are closely united in the fusion of iron.

According to the doctrine of concomitance, the bread and

[3] *The Church Teaches*: Documents of the Church in English translation, translated and prepared by J. F. Clarkson et al. (St. Louis, Herder, 1955).

wine remain what they are; but at the time that the Eucharist and communion take place they become the vehicle of Christ's real presence: Christ's body and blood, his human and divine person, are united to the act of eating the bread and drinking the wine of the Eucharist.

This final concept has sometimes evolved to the point of separating Christ's real presence from the species of the bread and wine in such a way that, in Protestantism, the holy supper has often become a kind of agape during which Christ's presence is affirmed. Consequently, no difference is recognized between Christ's promise, "Where two or three meet in my name, I shall be there with them" (Mt. 18:20), and Christ's words at the last supper, "This is my body . . . This is my blood."

Luther's concept appears to be much more faithful to evangelical truth. It is also close to the Catholic concept, stripped of a materialism that really has nothing to do with the doctrine of transubstantiation.

A contemporary Protestant theologian, Franz-J. Leenhardt, affirms that he can accept the doctrine of transubstantiation properly understood. He thinks that the word "transubstantiation" expresses a transformation without pretending to furnish an explanation for this transformation.

> It is useful because it secures two affirmations which are essential to faith and in which everything is summarized: 1) The substance of things is not in their empirical data, but in the will of God who sustains them. 2) Jesus Christ affirms in the upper room, in a sovereign manner, his will that the bread be his body; he transforms the substance of this bread (*This Is My Body*).

Leenhardt's is an isolated viewpoint. Nevertheless, it reveals the possibility of harmonizing two positions which were formerly thought to be irreconcilable. We can also affirm that

Reformed Christians who adhere to the Calvinist tradition, after having held the doctrine of concomitance which sometimes caused them to tend toward Zwinglian symbolism, have returned to a more Lutheran position, that is, a position nearer to faith in the real presence closely connected to the eucharistic elements of bread and wine. Thus, in 1931, the synod of the Reformed Church of France made the following declaration regarding Christ's presence in the Eucharist: "Believers can hold different opinions concerning the mode of the Lord's presence in the sacrament, but not concerning the fact of the presence itself, a real presence according to the Spirit, inseparable from the elements of the Supper in the one same act of celebration."

Recently an official commission of theologians of the Lutheran and Reformed Churches of France agreed sufficiently to make the following affirmation:

> The mode of presence in the holy supper is a mystery which cannot be defined; but we confess the reality and sovereign efficacity of this presence. The Lord's presence does not depend on the faith of each person, because Christ binds himself to the act which attests to his presence. Those who approach the supper with faith in this presence receive its grace. Those who approach it while refusing to encounter Christ in it receive their judgment from it.

We have just noticed a certain convergence in faith in the Eucharist, the sacrificial memorial and real presence of Christ, between Catholic and Protestant theological positions influenced by the biblical and liturgical renewal. Divergencies remain, but, rather than cause us to despair, they should stimulate us to research and prayer.

The greatest of these difficulties is our concept of the ministry or priesthood. Although we are approaching each other as regards one same faith in the Eucharist, we are still faced with the problem of ministry regarding who can validly celebrate the Eucharist.

In the Catholic and Orthodox Churches, the only one who can celebrate the Eucharist is a priest ordained by a bishop who was himself consecrated by a bishop. Some churches in Protestantism, such as the Anglican Church and most Lutheran Churches,[4] have an episcopal ministry, but this ministry is not recognized by the Catholic Church. Others, like most of the Reformed Churches, do not have an episcopal ministry in the Catholic sense of the term. Thus, Protestant pastors, whatever they are, cannot be recognized by the Catholic Church as ministers who can celebrate the Eucharist validly. Vatican II's decree on ecumenism recalls this fact.

This has a very direct effect on the problem of intercommunion. It is possible to imagine that the Catholic Church will one day give access to its Eucharist to all Christians who believe in the real presence. This is purely an hypothesis, but one which does not contradict Catholic doctrine on the priesthood. However, the opposite seems impossible. How can the Catholic Church authorize its faithful to receive communion from Protestant pastors, the validity of whose ministry it does not recognize?

We find ourselves facing a dead-end. Perhaps in the future, Catholic theology will develop a concept of extraordinary ministry which is the fruit of God's supplying grace. Such a theory would hold that God, in his mercy, supplies for the absence of apostolic succession, such as the Catholic Church understands it, in order to institute an extraordinary ministry. This is entirely a conjecture on our part. But, for hope's sake, let us recall that the text of Vatican II concerning the holy supper

[4] As opposed to United States custom, Lutheran Churches in Europe include an episcopal ministry.

celebrated by Protestants would have been unthinkable ten years ago:

> The ecclesial Communities separated from us lack that fullness of unity with us which should flow from baptism, and we believe that especially because of the lack of the sacrament of orders they have not preserved the genuine and total reality of the Eucharistic mystery. Nevertheless, when they commemorate the Lord's death and resurrection in the Holy Supper, they profess that it signifies life in communion with Christ and they await His coming in glory. For these reasons, dialogue should be undertaken concerning the true meaning of the Lord's Supper, the other sacraments, and the Church's worship and ministry.

Cardinal Bea continued this line of thought when he spoke at the Italian Eucharistic Congress in June 1965—thoughts which he took up again at Taizé during the International Youth Conference in September 1966:

> It is not up to us to scrutinize the mysteries of divine Providence and its merciful ways of helping and vivifying those who, in good faith, serve God as best they can. Everything we have said suffices to affirm that, for our separated brethren as well, the holy supper can be and is a source of unifying grace, though in a manner and measure known to God alone. It is a manner universal to all Christians: the more they unite themselves to Christ by eating his Body and drinking his Blood, the more we will progressively surmount actual divisions and realize the full unity to which everyone is called in virtue of Baptism.

After having emphasized the convergence which is presently taking place in eucharistic doctrine, we will now approach the problem of ministry or priesthood, whose ecumenical solution would be a key for access to intercommunion and the visible unity of Christians. Along with study of the Eucharist, study of the ministry is part of the wish expressed by Vatican II in its decree on ecumenism: "Dialogue should be undertaken concerning the true meaning of the *Lord's supper*, the other sacraments, and the Church's worship and *ministry*."

Priesthood
and Ministry in the Church

COMMON DOCTRINE AND PROBLEMS

The problem regarding the ministry is coming under fresh scrutiny today due to a number of present factors which lead us to hope that new ecumenical progress will be made in the dialogue between churches and in the projects for union that are under way. We would like to emphasize five of these actual factors which are shedding new ecumenical light on the problem regarding the ministry.

(1) Dialogue and ecumenical coexistence are showing us more and more how similar the ministerial fact is in the various churches. Whatever the doctrines or theologies of the ministries may be, the churches are being brought to recognize today that the ministries are an imperative fact to each one of them. The ministries appear under a great variety of forms, experience great difficulties of existence and live in considerable tension

between the theology professed and the reality lived. The great majority of the churches accept the fact of the ministries as a gift from God for the service of the church.

The "catholic" churches who have the doctrine of three ministries—episcopal, presbyteral, and diaconal—should recognize that these ministries are not being lived today as they were, for example, in the second century, and that through the course of history the episcopal fact or the presbyteral fact have presented themselves under extremely diverse forms. What church lives today the diaconal ministry conformable to its doctrine or its liturgy?

Haven't the "protestant" churches, whose doctrine is the diversity of the ministries—the pastor, the elder, the deacon, the teacher, etc.—reduced their whole concept of the ministry to that of the pastor? At present, the elder is seldom more than a lay counselor in the parish, the deacon exists little or not at all, the teacher is a pastor who has become a professor of theology. Where the episcopal ministry was refused, often for reasons more historical than theological, we find a practical or pastoral necessity gradually appearing under the form of a regional presidency or a superintendence.

Looking at the history of the churches we discern a kind of providence in the divisive ministerial fact, which always reappears, according to certain constant factors, through the different forms influenced by civil society and by the vicissitudes of confessional oppositions. Today, the churches seem ready to get rid of the nontheological factors to rediscover a doctrine and a common practice of the ministries in the light of the word of God.

(2) The great social evolutions bring all the churches to rethink the forms of their ministries so that they can better answer their vocation of service to contemporary Christians. A predominantly rural world, made up of village units, is evolv-

ing toward an urban civilization composed of a plurality of communities overlapping each other. The parish community corresponds well to the rural, communal unity; but the parish is no longer adequate for the pluralistic society of large cities, where a person no longer belongs to a defined geographical community but where his group derives from his work, interest and culture.

The concept of the ministries, in the service of man as he is and lives, must therefore be modified because of this social revolution. Today's great social evolutions are also bringing the churches to create new ministries adapted to modern situations on the basis of the fundamental ministry of the word, the sacraments and unity. The churches need courage and imagination in this creation of new forms of the ministry which are unknown both to their history and to their ecclesiology.

(3) The results of biblical and patristic research show that we cannot find in the scriptural texts or in ancient tradition ready-made solutions to the problem of the ministries. We cannot find, as such, in the New Testament the three classical ministries of bishop, priest and deacon as we find them in the doctrine or practice of certain churches. Between the *episcopê* of the pastoral epistles, the *episcopê in presbyterio* of the letters of St. Ignatius of Antioch, the episcopal concept of St. Augustine, that of the Middle Ages, that of eighteenth century Anglicanism and that of Vatican II there is a certain relationship, but we notice above all a considerable difference.

Neither can we pretend to read clearly in the New Testament texts the presbytero-synodal constitution of some Protestant Churches, nor can we affirm that the Reformed presbyteral elders or counselors correspond exactly to the presbyters in the Acts and in the pastoral epistles. The scriptural texts establish with sufficient evidence the existence of diverse ministries constituted by the Holy Spirit and the apostles. But the form that they took in apostolic times is due in large part to the concrete situations in which the Christians lived and to the heritage which they received from the Jewish Synagogue.

Contemporary studies concerning the meaning of the apostolate of the Twelve and their collaborators also renews the churches' reflection on the apostolic ministry and its continuity in history. We can no longer look upon the apostles as merely the nucleus of the whole church, nor make them merely the first bishops of the church from whom all others descend by personal and automatic succession.

We must recall here the diversity of hermeneutical options and exegeses in the New Testament concerning the structure of the church and the ministers. Our position with regard to the pastoral epistles, for example, is to see in the development of the ministries a providence of the Spirit where others see only a historical contingency, and to see a continuity between Paul's charismatic doctrine and the ministerial spirit of the pastoral epistles where others see only a contradiction. We must recognize that there are options in this matter which ultimately depend on the attitude one takes regarding the New Testament canon and its normative value. Our option, which proceeds from a conviction that the apostolic church described by the New Testament developed homogeneously, is proposed here as a working hypothesis. At any rate, the question is not one of reproducing as such the ministerial structures of the first century, but of finding those which are adequate for the church's mission today on the normative basis of the spirit which animated the first century structures. This spirit is none other than the Holy Spirit who distributes charisms and establishes the ministries.

(4) The renewal of the doctrine of the royal priesthood of all the People of God greatly affects the concepts of the ministries in the church. According to this authentically biblical con-

cept, it is proper to distinguish, without separating them, the priesthood of the whole church and the ministry of those who are ordained for the particular service of the church. Down through history the priesthood has sometimes appeared to be the monopoly and privilege of ordained ministers alone. This restrictive concept of the priesthood led to unfortunate separation between clergy and laity and to the equally unfortunate distinction between the church teaching and the church taught. Clericalism, from which all the churches have suffered in various degrees, is the consequence of this dichotomy.

Contemporary biblical ecclesiology makes evident the role of the entire People of God, of the whole church, of all Christians forming one single "laos," one same laity, in the exercise of the royal and prophetic priesthood. United to Christ-Priest, all the faithful constitute one unique priesthood (hierateuma, I Pet. 2:9), all the faithful are priests (hiereis, Rev. 1:6). The various ministers in the church are at the service (diaconia) of this unique priesthood of Christ and of the entire church. They are the ministers or servants of the royal and prophetic priesthood of the People of God.

The fact that Vatican II strongly developed this concept of the royal priesthood of the People of God, in the Constitution on the Church (chapter II), is very indicative of a general evolution. The entire problem consists in the distinction and union between the universal priesthood of the faithful and the particular ministry or service of this priesthood by ordained ministers.

(5) The fact that the role of the Holy Spirit in the church has been placed in greater evidence has also brought pressure on the churches to renew their concept of the ministry.

The relation of the ministries to the historical ministry of Christ and the apostles is being completed today by reflection on the epicletic function of the Holy Spirit who pours his gifts on the People of God, renews the ministries, actualizes their function, supplies for their indigence and unites in one same mission all of Christ's faithful servants.

Contemporary reflection on the charisms, on the prophetic character of the ministry, on the notion of supplement and on the recognition of all the evangelical elements in the ministry of the separated churches, is bringing the churches out of a too institutionalized concept of the ministries so that they can rediscover their pneumatic and charismatic character. In this context, dialogue between the historical churches on the one hand, and the Quakers and Pentecostal communities on the other, assumes capital importance in our rediscovery of the Holy Spirit's presence in the mission and ministry of the church.

THE PRIESTHOOD AND THE MINISTRY OF CHRIST

In order to properly approach and correctly understand, in their relation to each other, the universal priesthood of baptized Christians and the particular ministry of ordained ministers, in the church as the People of God and in the world of today, we must first of all recall the meaning of the priesthood and ministry of Christ, prophet, priest and king which is the foundation and justification of every priesthood and every ministry.

Christ substituted himself totally for man in order to accomplish man's redemption. Christ did not come to meet man, who could hardly approach him, merely to help man to walk the rest of the way to God. Christ did not come to bring man the strength he might need to rise from his misery to communion with God. Christ took man's place to live totally a truly human life so that our definitive redemption would be accomplished in this perfect, human life which he lived.

It is by the communion between our sinful and weak humanity and Christ's holy and perfect humanity that we are taken up in a movement which tears us away from ourselves and elevates us toward the Father. Christ, the incarnate Son of God, lived as a man in order to come to tear us away from sin and from ourselves, to live in us by the Holy Spirit, to take us up in his love and obedience toward the Father.

It is in this perspective of the Son's Incarnation, his total participation in our humanity and his substitution for man in order to take man up from misery to glory, that we must understand Christ's unique priesthood. His priesthood can reconcile us with God and reestablish us in perfect communion with him. Human priesthood and the priesthood of the Old Covenant were unable to obtain peace with God for us, because the priests of this earth are subject to the same weaknesses as other men. Only Christ, the "holy, innocent and uncontaminated high priest," could offer the perfect and definitive sacrifice pleasing to God and thus obtain redemption for us. Christ entered the heavenly sanctuary to present there to the Father the memorial of the sacrifice of the cross and, in this way, to become a living intercession for us (Heb. 9:24-28).

To be sure, this concept of Christ as high priest is not the first one we come across in the New Testament. It is unknown to the Synoptics. St. John probably alludes to it in the episode of the tunic without a seam: the crucified Christ had worn the same kind of garment as the high priest (Jn. 19:23). It is in the epistle to the Hebrews, in an apologetical text addressed to the Jews, that this priestly concept of Christ's work is developed. But this in itself is of great importance to show that Christ constituted the end of the Old Covenant sacrifice and priesthood, and that the cult and ministry of the New Covenant are radically new as signs of Christ's unique sacrifice on the cross and of his unique priesthood.

The royal and prophetic priesthood of the church and of the ministry in the church are therefore possible only in communion, through the Holy Spirit, with the unique and perfect priesthood and ministry of Christ, the mediator who is man and God, priest and king. They are possible only as signs and instruments of the unique and perfect priesthood and ministry of Christ who became man to raise us up all the way to God. They have no consistency or value in themselves; they exist only by the priesthood and ministry of Christ the mediator, which they signify and serve, represent and effect.

Christ's entire life was a perpetual service of God and men. On the eve of his passion, with the gesture of washing feet, he signified the whole purpose of his life and death, which was to serve God and men. Fully conscious of all his divine authority, "knowing that the Father had put everything into his hands, and that he had come from God and was returning to God" (Jn. 13:3), certain of his function as "the apostle and the high priest of our religion" (Heb. 3:1), as envoy from God to men and as the representative of men before God, Christ nevertheless wanted to be among his own like him who serves. Conscious of the fullness of power he possessed as envoy of God (apostle) and as the representative of men (priest), he wanted to reveal to his apostles how they could become the signs and instruments of this unique apostolate and this unique priesthood to which the Father appointed him. So he washed and wiped the feet of each one of them.

At Peter's second refusal, Jesus replied, "If I do not wash you, you can have nothing in common with me" (Jn. 13:8). Peter had to accept this gesture of charity and humility in order to participate in Christ's life and ministry. He could not, as an apostle, be a sign and instrument of Christ's ministry in the church unless he agreed to participate totally in his Master's humiliation, service and sacrifice. As a minister of the church, Peter had to be in full communion with the Master who washes his followers' feet as an act of humble, willing and sacrificial charity.

After he instituted the Eucharist, Christ showed the apostles what an authority of service means: "The greatest among you must behave as if he were the youngest, the leader as if he were the one who serves" (*diaconôn*, Lk. 22:26). And he declares of himself: "Here am I among you as one who serves!" (*diaconôn*, Lk. 22:27). Jesus designates himself here as the deacon of the apostles; and the ministers of the church, according to the Master's example and in order to share in his unique ministry, must serve as deacons to their brothers. The greater an authority is in the church, the greater the humility and generous spirit of service and sacrifice that should be found in those who are called to exercise this authority, not as kings, but as deacons (Lk. 22:25). St. Peter writes: "Be shepherds of the flock of God that is entrusted to you: . . . Never be a dictator over any group that is put in your charge, but be an example that the whole flock can follow" (I Pet. 5:2-3).

If the Lord and Master of the church wanted to be a willing and humble deacon, the apostles and ministers of the church should do the same in order to truly exercise Christ's ministry. It is then that the ministers of the church are true signs and instruments of Christ's ministry and they can then believe in their Master's word: "Whoever welcomes the one I send welcomes me . . . Anyone who listens to you listens to me" (Jn. 13:20; Lk. 10:16).

The priesthood and ministry of Christ, in which the royal and prophetic priesthood of all Christians and the ministry in the church participate, has often been designated by the titles of "prophet, priest and king." These titles summarize the various aspects of Christ's priesthood and ministry by connecting them to the Old Covenant where these three functions manifest

God's action in and by means of his people. In this way, Christ appears as the Messiah who fulfills the Old Covenant's three-fold function symbolized in the persons of Moses, the prophet, Aaron, the priest, and David, the king. Christ is the perfect successor of Moses and the prophets, of Aaron and the priests, and of David and the kings of the Old Covenant; he accomplishes definitively the work which they inaugurated in the service of the living God. After Christ, there is no more prophet, priest or king in the Old Covenant sense; there is, rather, a prophetic, priestly, and royal people, who are the entire church, and ministers, who are signs and instruments of the unique prophet, priest and king: Christ.

This schema of Christ's threefold office, which has been used extensively in ecumenical discussions on the ministry, should not be exclusive, because it can lead to an overly simplified idea of Christ's work. While recognizing its value and usefulness, we must apply it in a way which completes and enriches the many ministerial titles which Christ has in the New Testament.

On the occasion of Christ's baptism in the Jordan, the Father bestowed on his well-beloved Son a perfect anointing in the power of the Holy Spirit. He was consecrated as the Anointed of God, the Messiah, the Christ. He received the prophetic, priestly and royal unction, so that he alone possessed definitively in the Holy Spirit the fullness of the Father's power over his people and over the world.

The three titles of prophet, priest and king are enriched by Christ's other ministerial titles which we can find in the New Testament. As prophet, he is also "the apostle of our religion" (Heb. 3:1): he is the Father's envoy or ambassador to let us know the word of God; he is also master and doctor (Mt. 23:8-12), because he shows us the way, teaches the truth and gives us life. As priest, he is also the suffering and sacrificed servant foretold by Isaiah (Mt. 3:17; 12:17-21; Is. 42:1-4), because he offers his own life in sacrifice (Heb. 9:11-12); he is also the intercessor of our prayer before the Father (Heb. 7:25), for he appears now before God's face in our favor (Heb. 9:24). As king, he is lord of the church and of the world, and he is pastor and episcopê of our souls (I Pet. 2:25) as the good shepherd who leads the flock of the church and watches over it with love (Jn. 10:11-16).

God's envoy, the apostle of our religion, Christ is also a prophet because, in the power of the Spirit, he proclaims God's word to give rise to faith. His ministry in Galilee appears as that of a prophet in the power of the Spirit (Lk. 4:14-15). He teaches in the synagogues like a prophet, master or doctor (Lk. 4:16-19). He gives to the law a spiritual and universal interpretation.

Christ the prophet, the man of the word of God, is also the man of the Spirit. He is a witness to the authenticity of the life of the Spirit. Religious institutions, legalistic observances, moralistic exigencies and ritualistic practices do not assure authentic communion with the living God. Only the life of the Spirit, which bears the fruit of charity, allows a true relation of faith with God. Christ did not condemn institutions, the law, morality, or the liturgy as such; they are useful as long as they are filled with the Holy Spirit, as long as they are "fulfilled" and interiorized, and as long as they are signs of, and not conditions for, the life of the Spirit. The Holy Spirit must vivify religion so that it becomes a living relation with God in Spirit and in truth (Jn. 4:23).

However, Christ's attitude with regard to institutions is clearly eschatological. The institution should not become a perpetual installation in the world. If it is penetrated with the Spirit, it is a dynamic sign of our provisory situation in this world whose image is a passing one. The institution, fulfilled and interiorized by the Holy Spirit, recalls simultaneously that Christ assumed our human nature fully and that we are strangers and travelers on earth waiting for the glorious appearance of Christ and his Kingdom.

Christ, the prophet, does not appear as one who denies and destroys the priestly and liturgical institution; he wants to fulfill, interiorize and vivify it by means of the Spirit and Truth, by means of the Holy Spirit and the word of God and he wants to orient it eschatologically. Simplistic oppositions must be abandoned; liberty-institution, spirit-liturgy, prophet-priest are oppositions that have no sense in the message of Christ. Rather, it is a matter of complementary terms; and the first vivifies and opens eschatologically on the second, which in turn serves the first as support and language.

Christ, the prophet, is the mouth of God who transmits his word in the power of the Holy Spirit to renew the life of the People of God. The prophetic ministry in the church, the sign and instrument of Christ the prophet, is the ministry of the word proclaimed with the power of the Holy Spirit. The Holy Spirit resurrects, vivifies, interiorizes and orients the ecclesial and liturgical institution toward eschatological fulfillment. This ecclesial and liturgical institution is the sign of the fidelity and continuity of the presence of the Lord in his Body, the church, and of the Lord who is, who was and who comes.

From the time of the transfiguration, which was a renewal of the messianic anointing of his baptism, when the Father again designated Jesus as the Messiah, his beloved Son on whom his favor rests (Mt. 3:17; 17:5), Christ proceeded resolutely toward the sacrifice of the cross. He directed his steps from Galilee to Jerusalem, the usual place for prophets to perish. After his baptismal anointing, he acted as prophet, proclaiming the word and accompanying this proclamation with miraculous signs in the power of the Spirit. After the illumination of the transfiguration, he also acted as priest in his passion and on the cross, fulfilling in this way his ministry as prophet so as to finally reach his ministry as king in his resurrection and ascension.

Christ is priest because he renounced himself, gave his life for others, walked steadfastly to the sacrifice of the cross, a sacrament of which he would give in the Eucharist, and lost his life in order to find it again. Just as they were called to participate in his prophetic ministry by proclaiming the good news of the Kingdom, the apostles were called to participate in his priestly ministry by renouncing themselves, taking up their cross, following Christ and losing their life for his sake in order to find it again (Mt. 16:24-25).

Christ is priest because in his passion and on the cross he offers the perfect sacrifice of his life for the salvation of men, and because in his heavenly intercession he prays for the application of this salvation to all men and for the sanctification of Christians. Christ is priest inasmuch as he is God's suffering servant who has become the immolated paschal lamb: in him, priest and victim are one. He is also priest inasmuch as he is the heavenly intercessor who appears now before the face of the Father in our favor; the glorious stigmata of his crucifixion are a living intercession before the Father.

The sacrifice of Christ, the priest, is not an exterior or symbolic sacrifice; it is the sacrifice of his person offered to the Father and to men; it is an interior and real sacrifice: "You who wanted no sacrifice or oblation, prepared a body for me. You took no pleasure in holocausts or sacrifices for sin; then I said, 'God, here I am! I am coming to obey your will'" (Heb. 10:5-7). The sacrifice of Christ the priest is the offering of his body to accomplish the Father's will. The sacrifice of the church, the prophetic and royal priesthood, will also be the personal and interior sacrifice of each Christian: St. Paul writes,

"Think of God's mercy, my brothers, and worship him, I beg you, in a way that is worthy of thinking beings, by offering your living bodies as a holy sacrifice, truly pleasing to God" (Rom. 12:1).

According to the symbolism of the liturgy of Expiations (Heb. 9), Christ's perfect and definitive priesthood was fulfilled in two stages: in the sacrifice of the cross, the total offering of himself, and in the perpetual memorial of his sacrifice for the salvation and sanctification of men. The priesthood of all the baptized is therefore a commitment, in communion with Christ, to a total sacrifice of our life and a fervent intercession for men.

Christ holds in the New Covenant the role which the king held in the Old Covenant. As God's Anointed, the king was the Lord's property and was filled with the Spirit. He represented the people before God, and he was the channel through which God blessed his people (I Kings 8). The king represented God in his glory and authority. Through his resurrection and ascension, Christ became Lord of the church and of the universe. He sits, as eternal king, at the right hand of the Father. There, he represents the entire church and intercedes for it by recalling his unique sacrifice. He leads his people and showers them with the blessings of the Holy Spirit. It is as king that at Pentecost, on behalf of the Father, he sent the Holy Spirit on the apostles to entrust them with a universal mission before men and to make of them his ambassadors in the church and in the world.

During his earthly life, the incarnate Son of God presented himself as the king-shepherd of his people (Jn. 10:1-18). In giving himself the title of shepherd, Christ revealed his identity as Messiah-king. He is the good shepherd because he gives his life for his sheep. Christ's priestly character, in that he was handed over and sacrificed for his people, is also implied here. The authority of the good shepherd is recognized because it proceeds from a generous love which sacrifices itself. The royal authority of Christ, the risen and glorified Lord, comes to him from the fact that he gave his life for all men, as the good shepherd for his sheep, and from the fact that he knows those who are his and they know him in a communion of life and love. It arises from the fact that men recognize his voice as that of an authentic shepherd and from the fact that he forces no one to enter the narrow limits of a human institution, but brings to faith everyone who belongs to him in the march of the People of God toward the eternal Kingdom.

Thus, Christ is the pastor and guardian (episcopos) of our lives (I Pet. 2:25); he is the good shepherd who sacrifices himself for the flock and who guards it with love against every evil. Christ's royal authority is founded entirely on his generous sacrifice and his vigilant love—it is pastoral and episcopal. The royal ministry in the church, sign and instrument of the unique ministry of Christ the king, pastor-episcopos, is a ministry of authority in the service of unity and charity between men—it is founded on generous sacrifice and vigilant love. The pastors-episcopoi in the church are authentic in their ministry only if they give their life like the good shepherd and watch over the flock entrusted to them with love and patience, according to the example of the "Archpastor," Christ (I Pet. 5:1-4).

The king of the Old Covenant was the channel through which God's blessing on his people passed. At Pentecost, on behalf of the Father, Christ sent the Holy Spirit upon the whole church in relation to its mission and ministry. The risen Christ had already breathed on the apostles to give them the Holy Spirit in view of the mission and ministry of reconciliation: " 'As the Father sent me, so am I sending you.' After saying this he breathed on them and said: 'Receive the Holy Spirit.

For those whose sins you forgive, they are forgiven; . . .' " (Jn. 20:21-23).

By the power of the Holy Spirit, the Father sent the Son into the world (Lk. 1:35); by the anointing with the Holy Spirit, he conferred on him his messianic function (Lk. 3:22); in the fullness of the Holy Spirit, he gave him his prophetic mission (Lk. 4:1,14-15).

The Holy Spirit proceeds from the Father (Jn. 15:26). Through the Holy Spirit and with him the Father acted in the Son in his Incarnation. The Father sends the Holy Spirit in the Son's name (Jn. 14:26), and the Son sends him on the part of the Father (Jn. 15:26). As the Father sent the Son and gave him a mission and ministry, so also the Son sends the apostles in the power of the Holy Spirit and gives them a mission and ministry, transmitting to them the power of the Holy Spirit on the part of the Father. The apostles receive, with the Holy Spirit, the mission and ministry of reconciliation (Jn. 20:21-23).

The church's mission and its ministry are likewise the work of the Holy Spirit sent by the Father and the Son. There is a mission and a ministry in the church only in the power of the Holy Spirit, on the part of the Father and in the name of Christ. The Holy Spirit gives efficacy to the word of God; he makes real the promise contained in the sacraments; he brings about the unity of the Christian community by filling it with charity. All of the church's mission and all of its ministry therefore suppose a constant epiclesis of the Spirit, a prayer that the Holy Spirit open men's hearts to the word of God and act so that the sacraments be the efficacious signs of Christ's presence, uniting Christians in one single body animated with the same fraternal love.

PRIESTHOOD AND MINISTRY IN THE CHURCH

In order to understand the originality of Christ's priesthood and its relation with the priesthood of the entire church and with the ministry in the church, we must attain a precise understanding of the theological vocabulary involved. To designate a man consecrated to a sacrificial priesthood, the New Testament applies the title of "priest, *hiereus*," in four precise and well-defined cases:

(a) For the Jewish priests (e.g., Acts 4:1).

(b) For the pagan priests (Acts 14:13: the priests of Zeus).

(c) For Christ (Epistle to the Hebrews).

(d) For all Christians (*hierateuma*: I Pet. 2:9; *hiereis*: Rev. 1:6; 5:10; 20:6).

Christ appears in the Epistle to the Hebrews as the perfect and definitive priest who has offered the perfect and definitive sacrifice. He is the completion of the priesthood of Aaron according to the unexpected order of Melchisedech; after him there can no longer be priests or sacrifices as they existed in the Old Covenant which he completed and finished. His sacrificial priesthood, unique and perfect, personal and interior, accomplished in the total offering of himself on the cross and in his perpetual intercession before the face of the Father, ends the existence of priests and sacrifices of the Aaronic tradition; but it continues to unfold in his Body, the church, in the form of the royal and prophetic priesthood of all Christians (I Pet. 2:9). Therefore, there are no priests, *"hiereis,"* except Christ and all the baptized.

The New Testament never applies the title of "priest, *hiereus"* to the ministers of the church. Even the Jewish priests converted to the gospel (Acts 6:7) do not seem to have occupied a particularly sacerdotal place in the church. The ministry in the church was exercised by apostles, prophets, evangelists, pastors, doctors, episcopoi, presbyters, deacons . . . (Eph. 4:11; Tim. and Tit.), but never by priests, *"hiereis,"* by men consecrated to a sacrificial priesthood according to the meaning of the order of Aaron. The ministry in the church is of an entirely new and original nature with respect to the sacrificial priesthood of the Old Covenant.

Christ's priesthood and the priesthood of the entire church is a function of sacrifice and intercession. As Christ offered himself in sacrifice for the entire world, each Christian offers his entire person in a living, holy and pleasing sacrifice, offering with himself the world in order to consecrate it to God in the Spirit and in Truth. As Christ intercedes before the face of the Father on behalf of all men, so each Christian intercedes for all men so that they may find salvation and happiness in Jesus Christ. Christ's priesthood and the royal and prophetic priesthood of the entire People of God therefore has as its essential function the consecration of the world to God in sacrifice and intercession. This priesthood exists for the world and for all men; it is a priesthood constituting the mission of Christ and the church in the world. All Christians are priests in the communion of the Christ-priest, not for themselves or for the church, but for the world and in the world.

Christ's ministry and the ministry in the church has as its function to build and sanctify the Christian community by the word of God and the signs or sacraments of his presence and action, as well as by the power of his Spirit in the service of charity and unity. Christ proclaimed the good news of the Kingdom of God, performed signs of the presence and work of God and exercised the authority of the Holy Spirit in order to rouse love and unity among his disciples. Likewise, the ministry in the church, which is Christ's ministry through his consecrated ministers, proclaims the gospel, performs the sacraments and exercises authority in order to serve charity and unity in the People of God. The ministry of Christ and the ministry in the church has, therefore, as its essential function the building and sanctification of the People of God by means of the word, the sacraments and authority: "To some, Christ's gift was that they should be apostles; to some, prophets; to some, evangelists; to some, pastors and teachers; so that the saints together make a unity in the work of service (diaconia), building up the body of Christ . . ." (Eph. 4:11-12). This ministry exists for the church and for all Christians; it constitutes the building of the Body of Christ, the church, by its Head, the glorious Christ (Eph. 4:13). Some Christians are ministers in the communion of Christ, namely, the deacon, pastor and episcopos (Jn. 13:17; Lk. 22:26-27; Jn. 10:11; I Pet. 2:25; 5:1-14); they are chosen, called and ordained by Christ and given by him to the church to construct the Body of Christ, to build and to sanctify the People of God by means of the word, the sacraments and the Spirit of strength, love and wisdom (II Tim. 1:7).

The royal and prophetic priesthood of the entire People of God—both for the world and the ministry ordained in the church to build up the Body of Christ—have as their end the praise and glory of God. The universal priesthood offers up the world to consecrate it to God in sacrifice and intercession so that it may glorify the Lord on the day of his visitation (I Pet. 2:4-12). The ordained ministry builds up the Body of Christ so that it may become ever better the royal and prophetic priesthood which offers the sacrifices of the Spirit pleasing to God through Jesus Christ (I Pet. 2:5). The universal priesthood and the ordained ministry have, therefore, one same end: the praise and glory of God. This is why they find their most profound unity in the worship rendered to God, especially in the Eucharist which realizes the communion of Christ's priesthood and ministry with the priesthood and ministry of the church.

Indeed, it is in the Eucharist, the gift of Christ's real presence, that each Christian offers himself in living, holy and pleasing sacrifice in union with the heavenly Intercessor; and it is in the Eucharist that the ministry is accomplished in the church by means of the proclamation of the word of God, the celebration of the sacrament of Christ's gift and sacrifice and the uniting of the Christian community into one body under the authority of the Pastor and Episcopos of our lives, symbolized in the presidency of the ministers of the church.

The universal priesthood of the People of God and the ordained ministry in the church exist, live and act inasmuch as they are a participation in Christ's priesthood and ministry and are in communion with him. Therefore, the mystery of participation and communion with Christ in his priesthood and ministry is the foundation of the priesthood of the entire church and of the ministry in the church. They are Christ's signs and instruments in the world and in the church.

By its participation and its communion with Christ as prophet, priest and king, the church as a whole, indeed each individual Christian, is a sign and instrument of the royal and prophetic priesthood of the Lord in the world. It constitutes a chosen race, a royal priesthood, a holy nation, a people devoted to the praise of him who has called us from the darkness to his admirable light to offer spiritual sacrifices pleasing to God through Jesus Christ, and to set a good example in the midst of the nations so that in seeing good works they may glorify God on the day of his visitation (I Pet. 2:9; 5:12). Christ, therefore, uses his Body, the church, as a sign and an instrument to proclaim the gospel in the world, to offer sacrifices to the Father according to the Spirit and to attract the world to God's glorification by means of the holiness of the Christian life.

By their participation and their communion with Christ,

deacon, pastor and episcopos, the ministers in the church, are signs and instruments of the Lord's ministry in the church. They constitute a college of ministers (I Tim. 4:14), chosen, called and ordained by God to be given to the church and to serve it, to organize and stimulate the royal and prophetic priesthood of the faithful and to build up the community of the Body of Christ. They do all this by proclaiming the word of God, celebrating the sacraments and by exercising the authority of the Holy Spirit to serve charity and unity among the People of God. Therefore, Christ uses ministers in the church as signs and instruments by which he himself can proclaim his word in the church, celebrate the sacraments of his presence and action, and exercise his authority as Pastor and Episcopos in the power of the Spirit, in order to stimulate charity and fortify unity among the People of God.

Since the time of Pentecost, the Holy Spirit has poured his gifts upon the church. He creates faith in the heart of Christians, attaches them to Christ and to his Body in baptism and enables them to understand the word of God. He animates their charity and welds their unity in the church and gives them his strength to witness to Christ in the world. The Holy Spirit gives charisms to some for the sake of the ministry in the church (I Cor. 12:4-11). The Holy Spirit distributes charisms, according to his wisdom, with great diversity, with due regard for the diversity of the ministries. The church is charged with recognizing and organizing these charisms, for the Spirit manifests himself for the sake of the common good (I Cor. 12:7). In this light the church recognizes that God has given to and established in it primarily the apostles, secondly the prophets, thirdly the doctors and finally the gifts of power together with the charisms of healing, helping, governing and speaking in tongues (I Cor. 12:27-28; Eph. 4:11-12). The Holy Spirit distributes charisms according to his wisdom; but, because the

church is the Body of Christ, he also establishes ministries that
correspond to these charisms in an order conducive to the common good. The Holy Spirit is at the origin of both the diversity
of the charisms and the organization of the ministries for the
purpose of constructing the Body of Christ. It is always the
same Spirit who acts in each charism and in each ministry (I
Cor. 12:4-6) to build up the Body of Christ. No contradiction
can be possible between a charismatic or pneumatic concept of
the church and a ministerial or institutional one. The two most
important Pauline texts regarding the ministries in the church
are categoric: the Holy Spirit gives charisms and ministries, he
organizes charisms and ministries (Eph. 4:11-12), he establishes the charismatic ministries (I Cor. 12:28). There is only
one Body and one Spirit (Eph. 4:4); there can be no contradiction between the Holy Spirit's distribution of charisms according to his wisdom and the organization of the ministries in
the Body of Christ. A ministry in the Body of Christ supposes a
charism from the Holy Spirit; the charism from the Holy Spirit
is given for the establishment of a ministry in the Body of
Christ.

Therefore, theologically, there is no contradiction between
the Body and the Spirit, between the ministries and charisms;
each exists for the other, for the sake of the common good and
to build up the church. Nevertheless, we must admit that the
churches have not always maintained this equilibrium in practice. One church, more anxious about the organization of the
Body and the order of ministers, comes to distrust the liberty of
the Spirit, forgets the need for charisms, closes itself against
prophetic renewal and dries up what would otherwise be a
fertile diversification of the ministries. Another church, more
sensitive to the life of the Spirit and to the distribution of charisms, comes to distrust the church as an institution, neglects the
need for ministries and hinders the organizing of charisms into

ordained ministries. It is clear that, according to St. Paul, neither of these extreme positions is correct; each is wrong precisely in its contempt for the elements it distrusts. The ecumenical truth of ecclesiology is found in an equilibrium between a just recognition of charisms, the liberty of the Spirit, the prophetic Spirit and the diversity of the ministries on the one hand, and a healthy concept of the ministry, the institution, continuity and ordination on the other.

Because the greater tendency in the church, as in society, is to become over-institutionalized in the organization of its ministries and, in this way, lose its charismatic and prophetic spirit, God maintains beside it Christian communities who refuse the ministerial institution on behalf of spiritual liberty. By their presence the church is held constantly attentive to the work of the Holy Spirit, who distributes charisms according to his wisdom and makes the prophetic call resound where he wishes for the good of the Body of Christ. May the church ever recognize the providential role of these communities and judge them, not according to the criteria of its theology or its canon law, but according to the fruits of the Spirit they bear!

Just as it is true that the ministries in the church correspond to charisms of the Holy Spirit and, therefore, that every true ministry is charismatic, it is equally true that the ministries do not have a monopoly on the charisms. The charisms are bestowed on the entire church, on all of the People of God, on all of the royal and prophetic priesthood of the baptized. Each Christian receives those gifts of the Holy Spirit which are necessary for his priesthood as a baptized person, for his witness in the world and for his service in the church. The priesthood of the baptized is charismatic. But each baptismal charism does not necessarily have a corresponding ministry. The ordained ministry in the church is the fruit of a particular vocation.

THE MINISTRY OF THE APOSTLES

The college of the twelve apostles is not only the fundamental nucleus of the entire church, but also the initial college of ministers in the church. Christ founded the ministry in the church when he instituted the college of the twelve apostles to whom he confided a mission as ambassadors in his name. In the institution of the college of the Twelve there are intransmissible elements and transmissible elements. The Twelve represent the new Israel, they replace the twelve tribes of the People of God, they are the foundation of the church, because they were eyewitnesses to the life, passion and resurrection of Christ. This aspect of the apostolic ministry is intransmissible. But the apostles were sent by Christ into the world with the mission to preach the gospel and to baptize, to celebrate the Eucharist and to impose their hands so as to give the Holy Spirit, to remit the sins of men and to gather the church together and build it up. These elements of their ministry were transmitted to others, to their immediate collaborators and to the presbyters, episcopoi and deacons whom they instituted in the local churches.

The mission of the Twelve is unique, inasmuch as they are the foundation and first authorities of the church; but it is extended to others, inasmuch as they are Christ's ambassadors sent to proclaim in his name the coming of the Kingdom of God (Lk. 10:9). The apostles and the ministers who succeed them are the envoys of Christ (Jn. 20:21-22). The Father sent the Son with the mission to proclaim the gospel in the power of the Spirit and to live, die and rise for the salvation of all men. In line with this mission which the Son received from the Father in the power of the Spirit, the Son, in turn, sent the apostles and their successors, giving them the Spirit to proclaim salvation in the world. The apostles and the ministers who succeed them are Christ's ambassadors: they can speak and act in his name and they are the signs and instruments of his word, presence and action in the world. Before his ascension, Christ, by his power in heaven and on earth, gave to the apostles the plenipotentiary mission of representing him before mankind until the end of the world; he assured them of his presence among them, and he commanded them to preach, baptize and make disciples of all nations (Mt. 28:18-20).

In their prophetic ministry of proclaiming the gospel, the apostles and the ministers who succeed them are assured by the promise that Christ is present by his word in their word: He said to the Seventy, "Anyone who listens to you listens to me" (Lk. 10:16; cf. Mt. 10:40-42; Mk. 9:35-37; Lk. 9:46-48; Jn. 13:20). Whoever welcomes an apostle or a minister as an ambassador sent by Christ and whoever listens to him as to one proclaiming Christ's word, welcomes and listens to Christ himself. To reject him is to reject Christ and the Father who sent him. But the apostles and ministers are assured of this authority of Christ only on the condition that they be "little ones," "servants," persons who are humble (Mt. 10:40-42; Mk. 9:33-37; Lk. 9:46-48). "For the least among you all," Christ told them, "that is the one who is great" (Lk. 9:48). The apostle, or the minister, who represents Christ and speaks in his name has authority from Christ only if he places himself among the least and makes himself the servant (the deacon) of all (Mk. 9:35). Humility and authority necessarily go together for the apostle and the minister. To represent the authority of Christ, it is necessary to represent the service and humility of Christ the deacon (Jn. 13:14-16).

Christ also promised to the apostles and to the ministers who would succeed them that he would act with them in other things besides the prophetic proclamation of the gospel. He promised that he would be with them in the signs of his presence and of his work; in baptism in the name of the Triune

God (Mt. 28:19), in the Eucharist of his Body and Blood
(Mt. 26:26; etc.), the imposition of hands which transmits the
Holy Spirit (Acts 8:17; I Tim. 4:14), the absolution which
frees from sin (Jn. 20:23) and the unction which fortifies or
heals the sick (Mk. 6:13; Jam. 5:14). In all these acts of the
church it is Christ himself who acts through his ministers. It is
Christ who makes us pass through baptism in his death for the
sake of the resurrection and Christ again who presides at the
meal of the Eucharist where he gives himself as food; it is
Christ who transmits the Holy Spirit and Christ who unbinds
the sinner and heals the sick.

This charge, given to the apostles and to the ministers who
would succeed them, to represent as ambassadors the word,
presence and action of God himself, was summarized by Christ
in his promise to Peter and then to all the apostles and ministers: "I will give you the keys of the kingdom of heaven: whatever you bind on earth shall be considered bound in heaven;
whatever you loose on earth shall be considered loosed in
heaven" (Mt. 16:19; 18:18). Peter, as first among the apostles, but in solidarity with all of them, received the keys of the
steward of the house of God. His ministry confers on him the
charge and service of caring for and dispensing the goods of his
house in the name of his Master. It is the charge and service of
releasing men who are bound by sin by means of the liberating
power of the gospel. This charge and service apply to the total-
ity of the ministry in the church; together they sum up the
charges and services of the word, the sacraments and the authority which devolve from the ministry in the name of Christ.
Each minister participates in this charge and this service of the
gospel which liberates: in this ministry of the word of God, of
the sacraments of Christ's presence and action and of the authority of the Spirit ordering the church. Each ministry does
not participate equally in this charge and this service, but only

according to the responsibility God has invested in it. Christ promised the ministry of steward first of all to Peter, as the first of the college of the Twelve, and then to the other apostles (Mt. 16:19; 8:18). There is only one single charge and one single service of the gospel which liberates and reconciles, but there is a diversity of charisms and ministries.

Peter's ministry, as the first of the college of the Twelve, is difficult to specify on the basis of the New Testament. Because of his faith in Christ, the Son of the living God, a revelation which came to Peter from the Father, he is the first stone in the construction of the church (Mt. 16:16-18). Christ prayed for him so that his faith might not fail despite his triple denial (Lk. 22:31-34). Christ told him, "Once you have recovered, you in your turn must strengthen your brothers" (Lk. 22:32). It is perhaps in this charge and service of strengthening his brothers, the other apostles, that we should recognize the ministry proper to Peter. Is this ministry transmissible, or did it concern only the person of Peter among the Twelve? The traditions differ on this point. Is there place in the church for the ministry of a pastor of pastors? According to some, each bishop participates to a degree in Peter's ministry in the charge and service of strengthening the ministers of the church confided to him. According to others, there is in the church a bishop who has the charge and service of strengthening his brother bishops.

In choosing the Twelve, Christ gave a foundation to the new Israel, the church. Just as ancient Israel was constituted from the twelve tribes, the church was to be the extension of the college of the Twelve, its foundation, initial nucleus and pastoral government. The entire church in its different parts and functions—the People of God and the ministry—can be found in the college of the Twelve. The apostles are at the origin of the church's entire existence. Furthermore, if the apostles are the initial nucleus of all the new Israel, as the People of God, they are also at the origin of the ministry in the church. The ministry of the Twelve is not only at the origin of the church, but, just as Christ continues to act in the church through the ministry as the unique prophet, priest and king and as the perfect deacon, good shepherd and supreme episcopos, so the apostles also remain present to the church to govern it as a college submitted to Christ. They do this by their testimony which resounds through the New Testament and by their prayer in communion with Christ who is the heavenly intercessor before the face of the Father.

Christ gave the apostles the mission to found and spread the church by means of their word which contained the word of God, by celebrating Christ's sacraments and by exercising the Spirit's authority in charity with a view to unity. Essentially, they were constituted missionaries, founders and pastors. It is evident that their mission as the first missionaries, founders and pastors, inasmuch as they transmitted the word of God under the inspiration of the Holy Spirit, remains unique, intransmissible and permanent. Their unique mission is consigned to the New Testament and preserved in it; nothing can be added to it under the title of God's inspired word. This witness remains living and permanent in the church. In his faith in the Son of the living God, Peter remains forever the stone on which Christ built his church; and the gates of the underworld will not hold out against it (Mt. 16:16-18).

The edifice of the church has the apostles and prophets for its foundation and Jesus Christ himself for its cornerstone (Eph. 2:20). But the apostles themselves enlisted collaborators. Part of their ministry is transmissible: it must be continued on the basis of their first and unique testimony as witnesses to Christ's life, death and resurrection. Other churches must be founded other than those which they founded themselves. In the absence of the apostles, these churches must be guided, presided over and governed by ministers acting in continuity with their apostolic mission, under the authority of their living testimony, as ambassadors of Christ the good Shepherd and supreme Episcopos.

The college of the Twelve was instituted by Christ as the foundation of the new Israel to accomplish the mission of the gospel and to found and govern the churches. But other apostles were added, chosen directly by the glorious Christ or chosen by Christ's apostles. Matthias and Paul seem to have been chosen by the glorious Christ himself (Acts 1:23-26; 9:3-5). Matthias' election manifests the unique importance of the college of the Twelve; Paul's shows that Christ foresaw the extension of the apostolate. The apostles can increase in number; they can institute apostles of the apostles, apostles through the intermediation of a man (Gal. 1:1). The extension of the church requires this extension of the apostolate. We can see in the institution of the Seven (Acts 6:1-7) and in the presbyteral organization of the Church of Jerusalem that the apostles intended to avail themselves of the help of ministers right from the beginning. With his election of Paul, Christ invited them to extend the ministry of the apostolate itself. There would be in the church not only presbyters and deacons assisting Christ's apostles, but also apostles of the apostles, auxiliaries and delegates of the apostles, with the apostolic mission to found and govern churches and with the ecumenical function of providing the bond of unity between the churches, in communion with the Twelve and Paul. For this reason, Barnabas, Silvanus and Timothy are explicitly called apostles (Acts 14:14; I Th. 1:1; 2:7); Paul calls Epaphroditus his companion in working and battling (*sunergos, sunstratiotēs,* Phil. 2:25) and Epaphras his fellow servant (*sundoulos,* Col. 1:7; 4:2-13). They are the apostles' collaborators, aroused by the Holy Spirit to share in the apostolate of the Twelve as missionaries, founders and overseers of the churches. We see how Timothy at Ephesus and Titus at Crete are charged by the apostle with a ministry of organizing the church and supervising the local ministers, episcopoi, presbyters and deacons (I and II Tim., Tit.).

Christ himself had sent the Seventy, in addition to the Twelve, on a missionary journey (Lk. 10:1-16). Their number is probably symbolic, to recall the seventy Ancients of Israel who were to share the charge given to Moses (Num. 11:16-17). Just as the Spirit came over the seventy Ancients, so the Seventy were designated by Christ; and they received the mission to proclaim the Kingdom of God and heal the sick and the strength to tread underfoot all of the Enemy's power (Lk. 10:19). Whoever would listen to them would listen to Christ himself (Lk. 10:16). It is not true to say that all of the church's ministry extends from the college of the Twelve. The ministry which Chirst instituted took form in the college of the Twelve first of all; then it took form in the group of the Seventy who were also charged with the gospel, like the seventy Ancients who, filled with the Spirit, prophesied at Moses' side. Therefore, when the apostles instituted local ministries for the needs of the local churches, they imitated Moses. They chose ancients to share their charge of caring for the People of God, to receive the Holy Spirit in order to proclaim the word of God and to prophesy; they imitated Christ: they sent out disciples with the mission to announce the coming of the Kingdom (Lk. 10:3). The apostles recognized that God had given a ministry to ancients, prophets, pastors and doctors and they gave them a mission when they established them in their charge by the imposition of hands, the sign of the Holy Spirit giving his charisms.

We can say that from the time of its origin in the institution of Christ the ministry comes under two headings: that of the Twelve, patriarchs of the new Israel, and that of the Seventy, ancients and prophets of the new Israel. We observe that in the early church the same division continued and diversified itself. The apostles and their collaborators, on the one hand, founded and governed the churches; the local ministers, on the other hand, constructed and presided over a local church. Among the latter were prophets (preachers), pastors (shepherds), doctors (teachers), presbyters (ancients), episcopoi (overseers), deacons (servants), etc. Thus, the ministry in the primitive church is simultaneously an extension of the apostolic ministry of the Twelve, which grew with the number of apostles' collaborators to found and govern the churches, and a distribution of the ministerial charge in the local churches among local ministers who organized and presided over these churches.

THE MINISTRIES IN THE CHURCH

The proper and essential function of the ministry in the church consists in the proclamation of the word of God, the celebration of the sacraments of Christ and the exercise of the authority of the Spirit. As a baptized member of the People of God, the ordained minister of the church also has other responsibilities and functions, such as prayer, hospitality and visiting the unfortunate. To be sure, he exercises these "lay" responsibilities or functions with his ministerial charisms, but they do not constitute the proper element of his ordained ministry. They are part of his existence as a baptized Christian.

The ordained minister in the church is first of all a servant of the word of God. He has the charism and charge to proclaim the good news of salvation, the gospel. He accomplishes this in liturgical preaching, catechetical teaching and theological explanation. Secondly, he is an officiant of the sacraments of Christ. He presides at the celebration of the signs of Christ's presence and action for the sanctification of Christians.

Thirdly, he is the representative of the Holy Spirit's authority. In his responsibility for a community, in his work as spiritual director and in his care for certain of his brother Christians, he manifests by his function the Spirit's authority over men in order to encourage their growth in charity and to maintain unity among them.

In order to accomplish this fundamental ministry of the word, the sacraments and authority, the apostles and their collaborators organized ministries in the local churches. These diverse ministries of the primitive church were inspired by the structures of the Jewish synagogue, but they took on an original character in virtue of the fundamental ministry which they had been charged to accomplish. The pastoral epistles enable us to grasp the profound originality of the Christian ministries. It is not a matter of sacerdotal ministries in continuity with the priesthood of the Old Covenant. There is a clear break between the priesthood of the Temple and the ministry of the church. The forms of the Christian ministry were inspired first of all by the organization of the Synagogue. The ministry of the Church of Jerusalem appears to have been constituted by a college of presbyters over whom James presided and who acted in communion with the apostles living in Jerusalem (Acts 15:4,6,13; 21:18; Gal. 2:9). At Ephesus, the church also had a college that bore responsibility (Acts 20:17). The same was true at Crete (Tit. 1:5, 7). It is possible that in these churches a purely presbytero-collegial system evolved toward an episcopo-presbytero-collegial system. In any case, as long as the apostles and their collaborators were living, they assured the authority of supervision in these churches (I and II Tim., Tit.). In the letters of St. Ignatius of Antioch, less than fifty years after St. Paul's death, we find that the churches of Asia Minor, including Ephesus, are presided over by a bishop surrounded by a college of presbyters and deacons. We find that in the local church the bishop represents Christ, the presbyters the college of apostles and the deacons are charged with the service of Jesus Christ (Magn. VI,1; Trall. II,1-2; Eph. IV,1). It seems, therefore, that quite soon after the death of the apostles and their collaborators, like Timothy or Titus, a local presbyter-episcopos was charged with their responsibility of governing the church. But it was an episcopacy exercised in the collegial communion of the presbyterate and with the help of the diaconate.

The presbyters are established by the Holy Spirit as shepherds and guardians of the flock of the church (Acts 20:17,28). There is communion between the ministry of the presbyters, shepherds or pastors of the church and the ministry of Christ, the shepherd-guardian of the flock and pastor-episcopos of the church (I Pet. 2:25; 5:1-4). They should pasture the flock and watch over it with all their heart. They should do this by setting an example for the flock, so as to receive the crown of glory when the Archpastor, Christ, appears (I Pet. 5:1-4). The presbyter is a proven Christian, probably of somewhat advanced age, a man with experience at any rate, an "ancient" in the community, who has received a ministry from God and has been "constituted episcopos (overseer, guardian) to feed the Church of God" (Acts 20:28). The word "presbyter" refers to the minister's experience in the Christian life; the word "episcopos" refers to his function as shepherd, pastor, overseer and guardian. The title "presbyter" signifies a state; that of "episcopos" signifies a function.

The pastoral epistles summarize the qualities of an episcopos in terms of equilibrium in everything, a sense of welcoming, the ability to teach, a gift for government and humility in service (I Tim. 3:1-7). These qualities bring to light some of the essential functions of the episcopos. He is the minister of the church's internal government and God's steward (Tit. 1:7).

He ministers the teaching of the word of God; for this he must be attached to sound teaching and conform to doctrine (Tit. 1:9). He is the minister of the church's external relations: he should be hospitable (philoxenos: the friend of the stranger), and non-Christians (those outside) should be able to recognize his human qualities (I Tim. 3:2-7; Tit. 1:8). On the level of the pastoral epistles, it is difficult to define the deacon's function in relation to the presbyter-episcopos. If we interpret the diaconate in light of the institution of the Seven (Acts 6:1-6) and the letters of St. Ignatius, we can see in the deacons' ministry a function of service in the church coming from Christ and subordinated to the presbyteral and episcopal ministry.

The apostles and their collaborators drew inspiration from the synagogal structure when they organized the ministries, while still safeguarding the fundamental originality of the Christian ministry. Likewise, it is normal that the church, while safeguarding what is essential in the Christian ministry, underwent the influence of certain social or religious forms in the organization of its ministerial structures. For this reason it is good to take note of the fundamental elements in the organization of the ministries which safeguard what is essential to the Christian ministry, so as not to risk losing them on the one hand or to believe ourselves connected with temporary structures on the other.

First of all, it seems that the apostles wanted their apostolic ministry of mission, foundation and liaison between the churches to be continued. A missionary, founding and episcopal (in the New Testament sense) ministry of liaison between the churches is, therefore, fundamental. An example is furnished for us by Timothy and Titus. Second, the pastoral epistles seem to teach that a local episcopal ministry to take care of local government, the true deposit of faith and the church's external relations is essential to the life of the church.

This episcopal ministry is not monarchical or authoritarian but is situated in the collegiality of a presbyterate and assisted by the diaconate.

Third, a presbyteral ministry is necessary to signify apostolic collegiality in the local church and to diversify the episcopal ministry and give it equilibrium.

Fourth, there should be a diaconal ministry to recall in the church that the ministry's service is characterized by the example of Christ's service. Finally, no ministerial structure should be closed or exclusive. The Holy Spirit should be left free to distribute charisms so that the ministries can be very diversified and adapted to all needs and to all ages.

Ministers and laymen constitute a single people, a single royal and prophetic priesthood, a single church. We do not serve their unity when we confuse their proper vocations and services. We emphasize and favor it, on the contrary, when we define precisely their respective functions in the People of God, the one royal and prophetic priesthood.

The ordained minister is first of all a baptized person, a member of the universal priesthood. His ordination which confers on him a ministry in the church does not take him out of the human condition of the laity. He remains in profound solidarity with the lay life and he is closely united to all of his brother Christians in all of his existence. These considerations should bring us to a question regarding the concrete and social life of ministers who participate fully in the human existence of all Christians and who are distinguished from laymen only by their vocation and ordination. In our times, for example, shouldn't a minister of the church have a secular "job" like every other man? Haven't we overly insisted, since the sixteenth century, on the university formation of ministers? Doesn't this formation run the danger of producing clerics who are cut off from the Christian people? And yet, the minister who has the vocation, charism and discipline of evangelical celibacy is not necessarily separated from other Christians by that very fact; he receives the grace of understanding with that of his particular vocation.

By his baptism, the layman belongs to the same universal priesthood as the minister. This priesthood should lead him to collaborate effectively with the minister in serving all men. Furthermore, the laity's collaboration in the ministry in the church should become evident in a presence and activity of the faithful on all levels of the ministry. Laymen should have their part in church councils on every level. Churches, in their constitution, should foresee the possibility of delegating certain ministerial tasks to laymen: the liturgy, preaching, catechesis, theology, the care of souls. Even though the universal priesthood exists above all for the world, laymen also have a service to perform in the church in collaboration with the ministers. Laymen need the ministers in the exercise of their priesthood for the world and the ministers need the laymen in the exercise of their ministry for the church. Their fundamental unity is constituted by one unique priesthood and one same service in the diversity of their vocations and functions. This unity is nourished in liturgical life, which associates ministers and laymen, each according to his vocation and proper function, in one same praise of God and one same intercession for the world.

As regards the fundamental elements in the organization of the ministries which serve the essential ministry of the word, the sacraments and authority, it is possible to establish today the useful existence of four principal types of ministers without excluding other types that the charisms of the Spirit might require in particular circumstances. These types of ministers correspond in part to the ministries as they presently exist in the churches.

Missionary bishops: These ministers should have as their primary task the missionary work and renewal of the church. Like the apostles and their collaborators, they should be itinerant and at the service of all the churches. Their work would be to stimulate the foundation of new churches, to encourage renewal in every domain of the Christian life and to establish bonds between the various churches. Their ministry would be one of conferences, sessions and retreats to convey information on the great modern problems to those responsible for the churches. Their function would manifest the church's primordial missionary character and the necessity of its ecumenical unity.

Resident bishops: Abstracting from the handicaps of history and the non-theological reasons in its refusals, each church should have, under one form or another, a ministry whose special work is the "episcopê," that is, the ministry of government, of safeguarding the true deposit of faith and of caring for the external relations of the local church with other churches and with the world. He is the pastor of pastors and exercises the ministry of caring for the souls of the other ministers in his church. It is not by his own personal authority that he exercises his ministry of government, but in the name of Christ, the invisible Pastor and Episcopos of souls (I Pet. 2:25). It is therefore by the word of God that he governs God's church. He is the ambassador and sign of Christ the Archpastor (I Pet. 5:4). This is why he should be capable of evangelical and apostolic teaching, of teaching the word of God of which he is the trustee and guardian (Tit. 1:9; I Tim. 6:20). However, he exercises his ministry of government "in presbyterio," in communion with the college of presbyters, in the community of the other ministers of the local church and also in communion with the other resident bishops of his country. The church, in its constitution, should foresee this adaptation of the episcopal government in the college of presbyters, the organic bond between this episcopal government and presbyteral collegiality. Such a system of episcopo-presbytero-collegial government is in accord with St. Ignatius' concept: "Be submissive to your bishop as to Jesus Christ . . . and submissive also to the college of presbyters as to the Apostles of Jesus Christ . . . Your venerable college of presbyters, truly worthy of God, is united to the episcopos like the strings to the lyre" (Trall. II, 1-2; Eph. IV, 1).

Presbyters: The presbyters are pastors in the church. With the episcopos they have the charge and service of the word, the sacraments and authority. They form the faith of Christians by the doctrine of the gospel, sanctify their life by celebrating the sacraments and build up their community in charity and unity. They constitute a presbyteral college over which the episcopos presides and with him they govern the local church. This collegial constitution of the presbyters should bring them to work together and even to live near each other. The evolution of modern society from rural to urban life demands new reflection on the subject of the collegial presbyterate. It is becoming less and less desirable that a presbyter live alone in a village. We must rather hope for the constitution of presbyteral communities, which will facilitate the ministry in common and from which the presbyters can radiate over a region. This type of presbyteral community is still more desirable in the city. Collegial life of the presbyters permits a better distribution of tasks, according to the particular charisms of each: one will devote himself to youth, another to students, a third one to workers, a fourth one to the liberal professions, etc. One will be a better catechist; another will be a good liturgist; a third one will have a taste for theology and teaching, etc. In modern secularized life, it will be desirable that the presbyters find professional employment as artisans, laborers, office workers, etc.

Then they will find in the presbyteral community the balance
and renewal necessary for them.

During the past few centuries there has been too much insistence on the intellectual and university formation of pastors
and this has contributed to the distance between them and laymen. According to the New Testament, the criteria for choosing presbyters are their experience of the life of the church and
their ability to teach the word of God; they are not depicted as
a theological aristocracy but as men who humbly serve the
universal priesthood of the laity. We must return to a presbyterate that is much more open, one that is less reserved to an
intellectual class. We cannot make a vocation from God necessarily pass through the channel of university faculties and di-
plomas. When the church does this, it deprives itself of a presbyterate which would be in closer contact with laymen of every
class. If the church wants to recover contact with all the various classes of society, it needs not only intellectual pastors, but
also worker-pastors, farmer-pastors, employee-pastors, etc.,
pastors whose formation was not progressively cut off from the
environment from which they came. Today, the church needs
ministers who are less clerical and less intellectual and who are
simpler and more common. This does not mean that presbyters
should not have a good biblical and theological formation; but
this formation could be shorter and concentrated more on es-
sentials, rather than being spread out to cover a university formation. A more advanced and more technical theological formation for some, who have a taste and ability for it, could lead
them to a ministry of theological teaching either in seminaries
or among their fellow presbyters and deacons in the form of
conferences or periodic reviews. We would find in this the ministry of doctor, not merely a university professor, but a presby-
ter-theologian in the service of his colleagues in the ministry.

Deacons: This ministry has been very neglected by the

churches and yet it is one that is essential to the life of the church. It is a ministry of service in relation with the episcopal and presbyteral ministry. Today, it is good to consider it in terms of the laity. There are many laymen who are called to take on responsibilities in the Christian community, in addition to their family, professional and social life. At a given moment in his life in the church, a layman who is responsible for a spiritual charge quite naturally becomes a servant who can be counted on definitively. He has been proven in his responsibility and in his life (I Tim. 3:10). It is only normal that at this stage the church propose to him that he become a minister, that it accept him as a deacon and ordain him in the diaconal ministry. Today, the deacon can be spiritually responsible for a sector of the city, for a large apartment building, for a rural village or for a professional group. There, he can be given the work of caring for souls, of visiting and of extending hospitality; he can preside over church meetings, preach, baptize and take on some of the liturgical functions in the eucharistic service. As well as being a minister of the church, he should retain the lay character of the Christian life in his family, professional and social life. He is a bond between the needs of the People of God and the ministry in the church. He is in close contact with the college of presbyters and the episcopos.

The ministries are the object of a vocation which comes from God. The Holy Spirit distributes his charisms among Christians, according to his wisdom, to give rise to various ministries for the sake of serving the church, building up the Body of Christ and developing the royal and prophetic priesthood of the People of God in the world. It is God who gives the various ministers (Eph. 4:11) and who establishes them in the church (I Cor. 12:28). They are personally called by the Holy Spirit, given and established by God, to be Christ's envoys and ambassadors and the signs and instruments of his word, presence and

authority as Pastor and Episcopos of the church (Acts 20:28; I
Pet. 2:25). But this intimate and personal vocation from God
must be recognized, built and consecrated by the church; this is
a necessary condition for its exercise as a ministry accepted by
the Christian community as coming from God. The Body of
Christ must recognize that some of its members are established
to express the service of its Head, Christ.

The church recognizes, builds and consecrates vocations to
the ministry in order to give them a mission in the construction
of the Body of Christ. The church does not give this mission
according to its own will. It is related to the mission given to
the Son by the Father, the mission given to the Twelve and to
the Seventy by Christ, the mission given to the Spirit by the
Father and the Son to descend on the apostles on the day of
Pentecost and the mission which the apostles gave to the first
ministers of the church. The mission which the church gives is
apostolic; it is the mission of announcing the word of God in
conformity with the doctrine of the apostles, of celebrating the
signs of Christ's presence and action in conformity with the
tradition of the apostles and of exercising the authority of the
Spirit in conformity with the practice of the apostles.

There is therefore an apostolic succession in the church from
its mission to its ministry. It is God's will that there always exist
in his church a ministry to pursue the work of the apostles who
were sent by the Son in the power of the Spirit. This mission is
authentic only if it conforms to the mission of the apostles, to
Christ's intention in sending the Twelve and the Seventy and to
the apostles' intention when they sent the first ministers of the
church. The churches are not in agreement concerning the authentic criterion of the ministry's apostolic mission. Some see
this criterion in the church's fidelity to Christ's and the apostles'
teaching, in fidelity to the word of God as it is contained in
scripture. They hold that the church is apostolic and can give

an apostolic mission to its ministers only if it is faithful to the apostolic doctrine. Others, while equally stressing the importance of fidelity to apostolic doctrine, also emphasize the importance of an episcopal succession which has come down to us all the way from the apostles. They hold that to be a minister of Christ, it is not sufficient to be faithful to apostolic doctrine and to receive a mission and ordination from a church which professes this fidelity; it is also necessary to be validly ordained in the historical succession of bishops. Modern ecumenical dialogue is tending to bring these two viewpoints together. Those who hold the first opinion do well to recognize the symbolic value which the historical succession of bishops has with regard to the church's unity down through time; those who hold the second opinion do well to recognize the spiritual value of a ministry ordained outside of this historical succession of bishops, in building up the church.

The mission is given by the church to a vocation which it recognizes in an act of ordination to the ministry by means of prayer and the imposition of hands. The majority of churches recognize in this act an apostolic institution which the church is obliged to follow: "You have in you a spiritual gift which was given to you when the prophets spoke and the body of elders laid their hands on you . . ." (I Tim. 4:14; II Tim. 1:6; I Tim. 1:18). Ordination to the ministry is a work of the Holy Spirit; and the Spirit expresses himself in prophecy, which is the witness of God and the church, and he acts by means of a gesture, the imposition of hands. In the act of ordination, the church, in a way, steps into the background in presence of the omnipotence of God's own designation and consecration in prophecy and the imposition of hands. The church acts as the Holy Spirit's docile instrument. The prophecy is the act of God's word expressing itself through the ministers of the church to witness to the fact that a member of the People of God is added to the ministerial body of the universal Christian community. The imposition of hands is the ecclesial gesture which denotes the gift of charism given by the Holy Spirit for the ministry.

Ordination is *a prayer* to the Holy Spirit that he bestow necessary gifts on the ministry. It is epiclesis of the Spirit on a man so that he may receive the charism of his ministry. Ordination is the Holy Spirit's *gift* of the charism asked for; it is his answer to the epicletic prayer. Ordination is *an engendering* to the ministry; it is the transmission of the Spirit's life and power, from generation to generation, by the ministers to the new ministers. Ordination is the new servant's *offering* of his ministry to God; it is the consecration of a man to Christ in the Spirit of strength, love and wisdom. Ordination is *a legitimation* to ministry in the church; it is the church's recognition that God is sending it a new ambassador of his word, presence and authority.

Ordination to the ministry is an ordination to the service of the entire church. It is therefore normal that the ordained ministry of one church be recognized by another church and that ministers be able to exercise their ministry everywhere in the universal church, while respecting local disciplines, of course. Unfortunately, this mutual recognition of ministries is not possible among all the churches, because of their divisions with regard to the doctrine of the ministry and recognition of apostolic succession.

Therefore, dialogue and negotiations concerning the visible unity of the churches implies a deeper inquiry into the apostolic doctrine of the ministry and a mutual reconciliation regarding ordination and apostolic succession. This requires from either side great lucidity in seeing what is essential and what is accidental to the ministry, what belongs to faith and what is the fruit of history, what are theological factors and what are non-theological factors. This also implies a spirit of sacrifice concerning one's own tradition and confidence in God whose Spirit breathes where he wishes when he distributes his charisms. Those of one opinion must enrich their concept of the ministry's continuity and validity by accepting this liberty of the Spirit whose presence and action should be judged according to the fruit which the ministry bears. Those of the other opinion must deepen their concept of the Spirit's spontaneity and liberty in the church by respecting the continuity of the faithfulness of God, who always wants to keep in his church a ministry which conforms to the mission of the apostles.

Above all, it is in an act of reconciliation of the ministries, of supplication that God complete, for the good of all, what he has begun in each one, and of confidence in the Spirit of truth and unity who supplies for our deficiencies and weaknesses, that the divided churches can obtain their visible unity. While waiting for this act of reconciliation of the ministries, wouldn't it be desirable that on the occasion when ministers are being ordained in one church, several ministers from other churches be invited to be present at the liturgy in order to concretely signify a spiritual commitment on the road to final reconciliation?

Intercommunion:
Various Conceptions and Observations

VARYING CONCEPTIONS

The convergence which is taking place on many points today regarding the doctrines of the Eucharist and the ministry is setting the problem of intercommunion between the visibly separated churches in a new light. Nevertheless, the divergencies and problems which continue to exist prevent some churches from accepting intercommunion. In discussing this problem, therefore, we must maintain a wholesome respect for these churches and their convictions. The Catholic Church and the Orthodox Church insist on total unity of faith and on the episcopal ministry's existence in historical succession, as necessary conditions for Eucharistic communion between divided Christians. It is in a spirit of total respect for these positions that we will discuss intercommunion for the churches who can presently accept it.

Because of the Catholic and Orthodox Churches' dogmatic positions concerning the Eucharist and the ministry, our remarks and discussions that follow are directed more to the other churches; but they intend to enable every Christian to better understand the difficult problem of intercommunion. Intercommunion exists where two churches, who do not belong to the same confessional family, agree to permit their members to communicate freely in either church.

If we use as our criterion, the degree of importance which the various churches place on the necessity of their concept of unity for the realization of intercommunion, it is possible to reduce the opinions on intercommunion to four major categories. We will give ecclesiastical titles to these four concepts, not because the churches who bear these titles hold these described points of view totally or integrally, but because traditionally they are the principal representatives of these points of view.

The "total" concept (Orthodox and Roman Catholic): According to this concept, the word "intercommunion" is meaningless because, properly speaking, intercommunion cannot exist in the church which is one and indivisible. There can only be a total communion which is at the same time a closed communion, implying a unity in doctrine and ministry or intercelebration between local or autocephalic churches.

This concept proceeds from a doctrine of ecclesial fullness in the one, single church of Christ. There is only one, single church, in the full sense of the term; and the fullness of the truth and ministry is found in this unique church of Christ. There cannot be communion at the same altar except in this unique church, and this total communion is closed to Christians who do not belong to that church. This communion is open, or total, only to members of the one church, whatever the local or autocephalic church to which they belong, on the condition that this local church is in communion with the one universal church.

According to this concept, it is impossible to understand or admit an intercommunion which would not be accompanied by total unity in one, single, visible church. The fact of receiving the Eucharist together at the same altar with the idea of again separating afterwards to return each to his own church, divided as before, appears to be a contradiction and therefore meaningless. Communion signifies a total unity which cannot be broken in any way. To receive communion in the one visible church is to affirm that one belongs to this church and can never leave it.

This ecclesial fullness implies total communion in the truth and an acceptance of one single ministry ordained in the episcopal fullness of the church. Communion in the one visible church presupposes faith in its orthodoxy and recognition that its ministers alone are authentically ordained in the charismatic, ecclesial fullness assured by a historical episcopacy.

The "ministerial" concept (Anglican): Regarding the possibility of intercommunion and inter-celebration, this concept lays emphasis on the unity of the ordained ministry and ecclesiastical discipline. Doctrine and faith certainly are not minimized, but, in practice, they are relative compared to the importance placed on the ministry and discipline. Concepts of validity and legality take first place where intercommunion is concerned. Only a church which has the historical succession of bishops possesses a ministry that is plenary and qualified to celebrate the Eucharist validly and lawfully.

A church of this type will admit intercommunion only with a church of episcopal tradition, understood as histocial succession, because a true ministry and therefore a valid Eucharist is found only in such a tradition. In certain precise cases, on condition that they are authorized, it will allow the faithful of other churches to receive communion from the hands of its ministers; under certain circumstances, it will practice a limited, open communion. This does not weaken its doctrine of the ministry because the minister is always one of its own and therefore validly ordained. In this instance, the eucharistic faith of the faithful occupies a position that is relative in comparison with the doctrine on the ministry and discipline. The doctrine is preserved; no particular conditions of faith or doctrine are asked of the communicants from other churches—it suffices that they be baptized and in good standing in their own church.

Furthermore, the faithful are not formally forbidden to receive communion in other churches, even non-episcopal ones. They are merely put on their guard against any inconsistency in faith that this might imply and against the confusion it might create. They are neither encouraged to such communion nor condemned for it. The decision is left to their own conscience.

The "doctrinal" concept (Lutheran): This concept puts the accent on eucharistic faith and doctrine. The condition for intercommunion is unity of faith in the real presence. The celebrant and the faithful should believe in the real presence of Christ's body and blood. This does not mean that ministerial discipline is minimized or that anyone at all can celebrate the Eucharist as long as he believes in the real presence. The accent is placed more on the truth than on the concept of ministry or discipline. Intercommunion will be possible among the churches as soon as they reach a doctrinal consensus on the Eucharist.

The "open" concept (Reformed): According to this concept, only Christ is master and host at the holy supper. No one can stop a baptized person who believes in Jesus Christ from receiving the holy supper wherever it be. Christ invites all Christians when the holy supper is celebrated; and all are bound in conscience to hear this call and to answer it. No ecclesiastical discipline, no doctrine on the ministry or other dogmatic concept can justify theologically the abstention of a faithful person or prohibition by a church. Only ecumenical respect can explain an abstention or justify an interdiction. This concept depends on an essentially Christocentric vision of the Eucharist: Christ is present; he invites Christians; he wants to give them unity in himself. Therefore, the holy supper is looked upon as a means by which divided Christians can progress towards total and visible unity.

Today, however, for the sake of ecumenical respect and so as not to compromise unity by confusion, it is better to avoid an intercommunion that would wound the deep convictions of another church. This is the discipline observed at Taizé: "We do not allow intercommunion at Taizé. Its practice gives rise to passionate oppositions which hurt the will to reconciliation among the baptized. In a way, it wounds the love which many have for the eucharistic institution . . ."

QUESTIONS AND REMARKS

The "total" concept: This concept is fully coherent theologically. It should be distinguished clearly from the three others. From a certain viewpoint the other three form a related group, because intercommunion at least remains a possibility for them. Despite the theological coherence of this first concept a few questions can be asked about it in terms of practice.

The churches that can admit only total and closed communion base themselves in this matter on an idea of fullness in truth and ministry. But do the faithful of these churches, who receive communion, always and everywhere believe integrally in this fullness? Isn't progress possible in faith and in the search for truth? If members of the faithful of the Orthodox Church are, in their faith, far from Orthodoxy, and are nevertheless permitted to receive communion, why aren't non-Orthodox faithful, whose faith is perhaps closer to Orthodoxy and who do not have a formal intention of opposing Orthodoxy, admitted to receive the sacrament?

In the churches who hold this "total" concept, doesn't there exist a certitude of being the mother-church which is accompanied by non-theological difficulties? This notion of maternity implies many positive values such as generosity, a sense of responsibility, anxiety for one's responsibilities, etc.; but it also implies sentiments which are purely human. Doesn't a "mother" church tend to set down strict conditions which more or less imply its conviction that unity signifies a return to the heart of the family?

The "ministerial" concept: The churches who hold this "ministerial" concept stress the importance of belonging to an institution whose continuity can be traced back through history all the way to the institution of Christ and the apostles (apostolic succession). Nevertheless, other churches who do not possess this historical continuity are not denied an efficacious and blessed ministry in the power of the Holy Spirit. It seems that a division is made here between the work of the Son and that of the Spirit. How can a church have an efficacious and blessed ministry in the power of the Spirit, without being somehow connected to Christ's own institution? Is it possible that Christ is at the origin of the valid historical institution of the church and, at the same time, that the Holy Spirit can bless and assure the efficacity of the ministry of a church which cannot legitimately claim apostolic institution? This seems to be a contradiction. The historical Christ who founded the church and the Spirit who makes its ministry efficacious are one. The doctrine of the Holy Spirit needs reexamination here.

The churches that hold this "ministerial" concept issued from a less radical reform than the one which gave birth to

Protestantism; they have retained a consciousness of historical continuity and a desire for it. Their own historical continuity has been contested and so they have had to justify it often; perhaps this explains the non-theological element which their attitude implies. They insist on the necessity of a valid ministry, because the validity of their own ministry comes under discussion. They have to defend the continuity of their history and they have to justify whatever rupture did take place.

The "doctrinal" concept: The insistence on eucharistic doctrine and faith which this concept makes is useful in ecumenical dialogue. Nevertheless, doesn't it sometimes hide an illusion? Are the churches who require faith in the real presence and even unity in doctrine as a condition for intercommunion sure of the faith of their own faithful? We can repeat here what we said with regard to the "total" concept concerning fullness of truth. A formula of consensus on the real presence does not certify that all the faithful have an explicit faith. The road to faith is a process. Isn't it better to manifest flexibility in this domain and to believe that liturgical and sacramental renewal, as well as ecumenical contacts, will do more for unity in faith than doctrinal agreements wrought with difficulty? We have a risk to run in our quest for unity and we must place our confidence in the Holy Spirit who is leading the churches more and more towards a deeper faith in Christ's real presence in the holy supper (cf. the reports of Lund and Montreal which we cited above).

We can suspect that this "doctrinal" concept was deeply marked by the discussions which took place in view of an understanding between Lutherans and Reformed Protestants in the sixteenth century and the importance that was placed on confessions of faith. Theological justifications and doctrinal agreements can here be a non-theological factor in this particular concept of unity of faith.

The "open" concept: This concept can proceed from a doctrine that the holy supper is purely symbolic. Once the Eucharist is emptied of its content, it becomes senseless to forbid anyone access to the fraternal meal. However, in the context of the ecumenical movement, it is rather a deep conviction of Christ's presence in the holy supper which encourages the churches to ask for intercommunion and open communion. But doesn't this insistence sometimes lead to an excessive facility in accepting any kind of intercommunion? Besides, an easy intercommunion veils the exacting character which a holy supper in common has. How can intercommunion be practiced between two distinct churches over a considerable period of time without anything changing between these churches with regard to their unity? How can we receive communion together with a firm knowledge that afterwards we will remain separated from an ecclesiastical point of view? Today, fortunately, the attention of the churches is being drawn to this anomaly.

Insistence on a broader practice of intercommunion is possible only if faith in the real presence and ministerial and liturgical discipline are considered with new seriousness. The churches that hold this "open" concept cannot legitimately pretend to be listened to if they continue to affirm their doctrine on the real presence, the ministry and their liturgical practice. Unless they reconsider their positions, these churches cannot pretend to call the other churches to an intercommunion where faith in the real presence, the doctrine on the ministry and liturgical practice are considered important. They can re-examine their position on these various points, in line with their own tradition, without giving rise to questions of validity or the mode of the real presence. It is a matter of ecumenical respect owed to sister-churches.

Finally, there are probably non-theological factors in this "open" concept. Whatever the real theological reasons for this position, can't we find a contingent explanation for this attitude in the history of the churches that defend it? They were born in a rupture of continuity with the past; they became diversified in a plurality of groups, of which no single one can consider itself "the church"; each one is part and all of them together are part of the entire church. Furthermore, it is normal that each ecclesiastical group, despite the division, feel the need of being open to others in order to live in certitude of the church's universality. Again, because its legitimacy comes under question, each group looks for recognition by others; and this is why it invites other churches to enter into its communion—this communion represents legitimacy for it.

We will not try now to show from scripture that one concept or the other is the more correct one. Rather, we will try to discern a spirit that can guide us in mutual comprehension with regard to intercommunion. There are two New Testament texts which are surely related to our problem: Mt. 12:1-8; I Cor. 11:26-34.

The incident of Jesus' disciples picking corn on the Sabbath is reported by the three synoptic gospels in almost the same words. The narrative contains an important teaching of Christ, who is Master of the most venerable revealed legal institutions (Mt. 12:1-8; Mk. 2:23-28; Lk. 6:1-5).

The disciples picked some corn as they passed through a field and this constituted work which was forbidden during the absolute Sabbath rest. The Pharisees reproached them for this violation of the Law; but Christ justified them by recalling the story of David and his companions who one day ate the bread of proposition which was consecrated to God and which could be eaten only by the priests (I Sam. 21:2-7). Ahimelech, the priest at Nob, did not have any ordinary bread on hand so he was willing to give David the bread of proposition consecrated to God. And Jesus drew two lessons from this episode: God wants mercy and not sacrifice (Hos. 6:6); the Son of man is master of the Sabbath. In God, love and mercy have absolute primacy. If we must choose between the observance of a liturgical or legal institution (sacrifice, the bread of proposition, the Sabbath) and the exigencies of merciful love (the hunger of men, for example), no hesitation can be possible: we must choose mercy.

Secondly, the reason given for this choice is that liturgical and legal institutions exist to serve man, to help him to obey God: "The Sabbath was made for man, not man for the Sabbath" (Mk. 2:27). Man's good comes before observance of the Law. And the Son of man, whose entire work is summarized in his merciful love, is master of the Sabbath, institutions and the Law. Man as such is not free to change legal institutions, but the Son of man is; and the Son of man manifests himself to men in charity because God is love. Therefore, whenever a choice must be made between charity and a legal institution, charity must rule as a sign of the presence of the Son of man; the love of charity and mercy is master of the Sabbath and of liturgical or legal institutions because it is the presence of the Son of man among us.

This supreme spiritual law is the foundation of the principle of "economy" in the tradition of the church, that is, the principle of charitably and mercifully applying or broadening an ecclesiastical rule. The ecumenical movement has reached a stage today where this principle of economy should be applied more broadly than ever, because unity, the actual sign of the Lord's merciful love, is pressing the churches to choose ever increasingly "mercy instead of sacrifice," the signs of unity in love as much as those of integrity in faith. The churches should ask themselves today whether a broader communion discipline might be the form that ecumenical "mercy" requires and that

they should show preference for confessional "law," because
the Son of man, who is master of all our laws, preferred it.
Shouldn't we see in our brothers, who are separated from us
confessionally, David and the apostles who are hungry? How
can we refuse them our "bread of proposition" when they ask
us for it, under the pretext that it is reserved for "our priests"
or that we have to safeguard "the Sabbath rest" of our ecclesiastical institutions?

After recalling the tradition of the Eucharist, St. Paul ex-
horts the Corinthians to observe eucharistic discipline (I Cor.
11:27-34). This discipline is concerned essentially with the necessity of "recognizing the Body" (v.29). This means that the
faithful must simultaneously recognize the Body of the historical Christ, who was crucified and rose from the dead, and the
Body of the ecclesial Christ, which is the Christian community
in unity and charity. The Corinthians gathered together for the
Lord's supper, but they did not realize the consequences of
unity and charity; they became divided and each ate the agape
for himself without worrying about the others. When we receive
the Lord's Body and Blood in communion, we are certainly
proclaiming his death until he comes, but this communion must
also be a recognition of his Body, the church, and of the unity
and charity which should reign in it. There is no true holy
supper, no true communion with the crucified and risen Lord,
which is not at the same time a sign of unity and charity that
commits every member of the church to visible unity and active
charity.

Eucharistic discipline implies a desire for authenticity. Eucharistic communion cannot take place between Christians unless they commit themselves to seek visible unity and to live in
effective charity. Eucharistic communion is possible between
the churches only if they intend to take every possible action to
end division and to concretize visible unity in every domain of

ecclesiastical life: in faith, the ministry and worship. Refusal of a decisive commitment to the fundamental unity of faith, which does not imply uniformity, and respect for a healthy diversity makes any participation in one same Eucharist a falsehood.

The fact of being near each other, praying together and knowing each other better, draws the churches together irresistibly and constrains theology to follow with its explanations for it. Unity certainly cannot come about by a confusion of doctrines, but it will come from our recognizing what truth we have in common. This truth, which is given in revelation, is explained, made explicit and deepened in tradition, which is the very life of the church believing, praying and obeying. Today, do not ecumenical dialogue, prayer for unity and fraternal life between separated Christians also constitute an integral part of this living tradition by which we are all enriched in our understanding of the word of God?

A day is coming when the progress of this tradition will find us near enough to each other to accomplish reconciliation in the unity of sister-churches. This unity in necessary, fundamental truth will allow an enriching diversity of theologies and liturgies together with participation in one same Eucharist. This is the truly luminous message contained in the meeting of Pope Paul VI and Patriarch Athenagoras I at Constantinople: unity in what is essential and reconciliation of sister-churches in one people constituted by baptism, unity and reconciliation in the universal family of the Father.

Part 2

CRISIS OF THE FAITH

The Crisis of Faith

Christianity's future, the possibility that it remain an essential value in the lives of men, depends on its capacity to become from now on the Christianity of the future, to effect what John XXIII called aggiornamento, bringing the church up to date. As Christians, we believe that the church will last until the end of time, we believe in the perpetuity of Christianity; but we must not delay its adaptation to the modern world lest we lose existing opportunities to evangelize our contemporaries.

We would have to be blind not to take account of the fact that the church, all the churches, are undergoing a decisive crisis today. Some, panic-stricken, are hardening themselves in a conservative and reactionary attitude. Others, drawn along too easily by the movements of modern thought, are ready to abandon values that have been considered essential since the time of the apostles: the great Trinitarian and Christological dogmas and even the very personality and transcendence of God; the church as a sacramental institution; the ordained ministry at the service of the People of God; both liturgical and personal prayer which might alienate man from his integration in the world; the very authority of scripture, the demythologizing of which leaves nothing but an unsure residue, etc.

Both groups, in the nervousness and precipitation that agitate them, think that this contemporary revolution of Christian thought is such as the church has never known before. But this shows a poor knowledge of history. Without minimizing the present crisis, but in order to stand back from it a little and to reanimate our hope in a solution that must come (God is faithful and he does not allow us to be tried beyond our strength), we should recall a few of the great crises through which the church has passed without suffering its foundations to crumble.

Early Christian thought has to pass through the Jewish culture, whose existentialism integrated in harmonious unity the God of nature and the God of history, the world of creation and the mystery of redemption, the realities of the body and those of the spirit, to the Greek culture which was much more intellectual and dualistic. Then, after meeting the Greek world with its inclination to theological speculation, Christian thought met Roman civilization with its institutional and juridical exigencies. With Constantine, the minority church was to become a recognized institution and was to superpose itself on a world which had persecuted it and which it had considered as the home of the forces of evil. Charlemagne, in his eagerness for centralization, imposed Roman theology and liturgy on the West, preparing in this way the inevitable rupture with the eastern patriarchs. What of the sixteenth century or of the birth of science in the nineteenth century which was to be the durable critic of religion? The church came out of all of these crises, upon which its history hinged, purified though sometimes wounded. We should not consider the present crisis to be any worse than the others. The church remains the community of hope; it knows that its Master overcame the powers of destruction by his resurrection; it believes that he is also Lord of the world and that through the events of history he wants to manifest to his own his will for today.

Communications, publicity and popularization render considerable service to contemporary Christian thought; but they also sometimes contribute to confusion. Theologians who would prefer to pursue their research in silence sometimes find certain of their working hypotheses presented as revolutionary theses destined to bring down the traditional institution of the church. What has not been published on Bultmann, Tillich, or Bonhoeffer? This surprises the Christian people, even scandalizes them, and they ask justifiably what is left that we can still believe, as they find themselves spectators while traditional theological propositions which they thought were beyond dispute are brought radically into question.

In biological and chemical research there reigns a kind of international discipline which does not allow the sale of new medicines in the pharmacies until numerous experiments have been made and sure results have been obtained and there is total assurance that they are safe. Research scholars constitute a kind of universal community of mutual aid realized by means of congresses and scientific exchanges. It would be desirable if, for the sake of the People of God, theologians would constitute a similar community and have enough pastoral sense not to popularize too quickly discoveries which are only provisory stages on the long road of research. To be a true scholar, the theologian should have a pastoral sense for the spiritual edification of Christians since he is doing his research in a subject which is the strength and consolation of the poorest. He knows that this truth, which is God, will always transcend his provisory approximations. He should have an ecclesial sensitivity since he believes that the truth is given to the universal community of Christians, that it is sometimes hidden from the wise and intelligent and revealed to the little ones, and that it is a truth lived by a people and not one possessed by an elite.

During the synod of bishops in Rome, in October, 1967, contemporary problems of faith were treated. Many concern the very center of Christian truth, such as the historical fact of Christ's resurrection. Others are more peripheral and demand long study before the church can pronounce on them with authority, such as the doctrine of original sin in its relation to scientific discoveries. It would be very unfortunate if hasty decisions were made. This is why the idea of having an international theological commission to represent all the different currents of opinion as demanded by many of the synodal Fathers, appears to be a possible fruit of the synod. Had it concluded with no more than this, in what concerns problems of faith, the synod would have accomplished a useful and durable work.

Indeed, it is becoming urgent that an international theological commission approach the diverse actual problems of faith because although it is true, as some have said, that these problems do not preoccupy all of the People of God, it is only a matter of time before the faithful are as informed as the theologians. There is one in particular which can no longer be avoided, and this is the problem of hermeneutics or the positive criticism of the language of scripture and tradition. The church has no need to be afraid of this problem. Hasn't the church always sought to express the word of God, contained in scripture and transmitted by tradition, with a language that corresponds to the one spoken by men in the age in which it is living? Our modern culture is very different from apostolic times, and it is normal that theologians seek to translate the culture of the first century in order to transmit to the twentieth century the immutable truth of Christ's gospel. This is all that hermeneutics intends.

The church knows that the word of God expressed in scripture lives in it in a process of living tradition. Like Mary, the church "ponders in its heart" the events of revelation, and in this way it deepens its knowledge of the word of God. The intense and patient work of exegetes is also part of this living tradition, and it is good that the bishops, who are responsible for the faith of the People of God, cooperate with them in this research. The bishops' role is not to hinder or to limit the scientific work of the exegetes but to bring to them a sense of the faith of the People of God. This sense, which is at the same time faithfulness to Christ and sensitivity to the world's criticism, has a role to play in the scientific research of the exegetes. Indeed, they do not study scripture as a simple human document but as the first literary expression of the revelation of God who still speaks today in a living way by means of the past events of the salvation which he continues to effect. The living tradition of faith, renewed also by the world's criticism, is a scientific instrument, together with history and philology, for the interpreters of scripture.

An international theological commission, formed of bishops, exegetes and dogmatic theologians, would be an 'effective instrument for theological research. It would promote the development of the faith of the People of God, a faith clarified by God's word as immutable truth, by new and modern expressions designed for true translation and healthy "transculturalization." This would be positive hermeneutics. Why shouldn't this work be accomplished in ecumenical collaboration, since today there is no church that can escape these problems of faith? We have certainly entered a period of mutual, interconfessional theological help in the search for an authentic expression of the eternal truth in a modern language which the world awaits in order to be able to listen fruitfully to the gospel of Christ.

The fact that the Third World Congress of the Lay Apostolate took place in Rome at the very time that the synod was in session illustrated magnificently one of the doctrines dear to Vatican II: the People of God. The celebration at St. Peter's on October 15, 1967, united the bishops and laymen in one prayer in the presence of the pope and an important number of non-Catholic observers. This or that aspect of this congress of laymen was criticized and continues to be criticized; but on the whole, it impressed by its faith, prayer and dynamism. The credo sung by the three thousand members of the congress at its closing session seemed to be a clear affirmation that it is on the basis of the biblical and traditional faith of the church that the laity wants to go forward. While the synod was studying the liturgy consilium's remarkable project on the breviary, the lay congress affirmed that the world needs priests who are men of prayer more than of any other activity however modern or effective.

At the crossroads in ecumenism, the theological and spiritual maturity of the laymen was striking. One thing of which we can be sure after this congress is that ecumenism will not be able to progress unless informed laymen are involved in the theological dialogue on the unity of Christians. The theologians of ecumenism often end up at dead-ends where the laymen's spiritual experience can bring enlightenment which will enable the work to progress.

Yet, although the will to renew the faith on the unshakeable basis of revelation marked simultaneously both the synod of bishops and the lay congress, we can feel a real suffering penetrating all of the Catholic Church. This suffering is shared with the world of war and hunger; but it is also an internal suffering of theological tensions, of misunderstandings between brothers, of acts of disobedience to God's word and of infidelities to the vocation which Christ addresses to us all. The Catholic Church is living through a time of purificatory suffering. Some persons are distressed by this; and yet, in this suffering lived in communion with the crucified Christ, there arises an immense hope of renewal, of unity and of evangelization.

As long as the church appears to be triumphant, and by this a stranger to humanity's vicissitudes, it is in danger of making people afraid and of keeping them at a distance. But when it knows suffering and a kind of agony, without losing the unshakeable assurance of its faith, it becomes friendly and brotherly, compassionate and attractive to men.

This suffering has a deeply ecumenical sense. Non-Catholics have sometimes feared the Catholic Church, because they judged it to be powerful and triumphant in a human sense. To be sure, there is a power and a triumph in Christ's resurrection which will always penetrate the church and without which it cannot live or subsist. But this power and triumph of Christ is accomplished in human weakness and at the heart of the church's purificatory suffering.

Suffering in this way, united to the crucified Christ, how close the church is to men and to all Christians, how brotherly and ecumenical! All the churches are undergoing these present difficulties, and it is a thirst for compassion and mutual aid which is attracting us one towards the other so that we can proclaim together Christ crucified and resurrected, present in his word and in his Eucharist.

It is in this light of the cross that the encounter between Paul VI and Athenagoras I will produce its fruit of unity. Both carry within them this suffering which Christ promised to every Christian that he would transform into joy, this suffering of the church which is again today giving birth to faith and unity.

The present crisis of faith, which promises for tomorrow a body of Christians purified and living in a fully assumed humanity, has as its essential causes the criticism of a secularized world and the prematurely divulged research of an insufficiently pastoral theology. It does no good to lament the situation; we must face up to the problems posed and seek the sense of God where the world wants to see nothing but the ridiculously absurd, where the conservative Christian is ready to stigmatize fearsome heresy, where the progressionist Christian runs the danger of enjoying the intoxicating adventure too much.

Since this crisis of faith, which commands the future of Christianity, reaches every church sooner or later, we must seek the answers together, that is ecumenically with a healthy attitude inspired by the word of God in order to face up to the changes we are living. In a first phase of ecumenism, we were able to look at one another, compare ourselves to each other, approach each other and reconcile ourselves without yet being able to unite ourselves; in a second phase, today, we should together look in the same direction: towards the world which criticizes us and towards the word of God which we should express, always the same, in a language which contemporary man can understand. Our modern ecumenism must be a mutual, spiritual and theological help to evangelize the modern world that God loves. This is perhaps the way in which we will progress into the last stage of visible unity for Christians, no longer looking at each other with love or suspicion, but looking together at the world for which Christ died and for which we, together, are called to sacrifice our ecclesial and confessional comfort, united so that the world may believe.

Cleansing Secularization

The criticism of Christianity which comes from the world has a twofold source: secularization and atheism. It is probable that the process of secularization will continue at an increasing pace and that atheism—if not doctrinal at least practical atheism—will be the real position of many men in the future.

Gradually, we are coming out of a long period in the history of humanity in which religion was part of life. Even for non-practicing Christians, God, some kind of faith, some prayer, especially at moments of desperation, had a place in existence. We are entering a new era in which natural man can do without God or any prayer. We must add, however, that this is especially true of North America and Europe at the present time and less so and only in the longer run for the peoples of Africa, Asia and Latin America.

The developments in science and technology will ever increasingly give man securities which will make recourse to a religious faith and prayer seem childish to him. Why should we ask of a God what we can obtain by means of technology? We are slowly finding the remedy for every sickness, so why pray for the healing of the sick? Even the discoveries of the psychological sciences and the ever increasing role of psychoanalysis are finding themselves being brought into question by chemical research applied to pharmacology. A neurosis may be cured by a certain dosage of chemical products without necessarily requiring psychotherapy. Won't it be possible tomorrow to make violent people peaceful, liars truthful and agitated people contemplative? Along with religious faith and intercessory prayer, man's moral will itself can be brought into question. Perhaps such predictions should be taken "with a grain of salt," but there is no doubt that the universe of science and technology, in its predictive precision, brings religion and prayer to failure.

We can be frightened by these perspectives of the secularization of a world which ignores faith and prayer more and more if we think that Christianity is necessarily bound up with natural religiosity, the religious attitude which rises up in a man when he is faced with the invincible forces of nature, fear of suffering, or the agony of death. But Christian faith, even if it has sometimes used the experiences of natural religion, is radically distinct from the religious sentiment which arises in a man's heart when he feels small and ignorant in face of the mystery of life and death. It is not up to Christian faith to combat or destroy natural religion; it can employ it as a language, but without identifying itself with it, up to the point where man wants to do without it. Indeed, Christ did not die for the salvation of religiosity, but for the salvation of man as man exists at each stage in his development. Although man may no longer be religious tomorrow and may no longer feel the need for a God and for prayer, Christ is there as he always is to save this man from his self-sufficiency, from his pride and egoism, to lead him to the generous and self-sacrificing love which unites him indissolubly to his brothers.

Secularization can become a purification for the Christian faith if Christians do not surrender before it and do not let themselves be won over by the spirit of the world. Their faith will be strengthened if they remain aware that the God revealed in Jesus Christ transcends all of man's aspirations and even his religious sentiments, and that he does not need natural religion to lead to faith and prayer those whom his Spirit assembles in the church of love. As early as the time of the Old Testament, we find this process of purificatory secularization present to some extent. From a religion of nature, where God directly maneuvers cosmic and physical forces to bring prosperity or calamity to men, there begins to appear, as a consequence of the revelations to Abraham, Moses and the prophets, a religion of history, where God, transcendent and personal, leads his people by forming the heart of each one by means of his word and his Spirit. Certainly, he is the creator of the visible as well as of the invisible. But, leaving the natural laws and their proper causes to function as he had ordained them to do, he is above all the master of human history, which he directs by converting the hearts of men, by inspiring human minds and by stimulating human wills.

Christ continued and completed this revelation of the God of history. Although he healed the sick, he did it above all to call them to the interior healing of sin. Although he performed natural miracles, he did it to furnish signs, comprehensible to the men of his times, of the much more important power he has to transform hearts of stone into hearts of flesh. Although he

gave bread to the crowd, he did it to make these men hunger
for the only bread that can satisfy them, the living bread which
is the holy word of God and the holy supper of his real presence.

Today and tomorrow, whatever there is of unnecessary natural religion in our Christianity will continue to be purified by
the secularization of the world. Because natural man will no
longer need religiosity and prayer, the Christian, touched by
the Spirit who opens up to him the way to the word of God,
will see his faith, purified of every too human interest, become
free attachment to Christ who has freely given his life through
love; he will see his prayer, turned away from an overly prosa-
ical petition, become a necessary contemplation of Christ in
order to work a transformation of heart and life in his image;
he will see his obedience, freed from a childish attitude, become an adult commitment to the service of Christ recognized
in men.

The secularization of the world will become purificatory for
the Christianity of the future by helping it to disengage from
natural, mythical and ritualistic religion to faith in God's word
and prayer in Christ's presence. Secularization invites faith to a
withdrawal from religiosity, to a change of language and expression which translates for the man of today and tomorrow,
who is without religious need, the eternal word of the transcendent and personal God.

We all have need for a renewal of faith, for a confirmation in
the fundamental truth which we proclaim in common. We may
feel a kind of sadness overcoming us when we hear essential
points in the gospel being brought into question here or there,
if we are not penetrated by the hope which, through the under-
standable upheavals of today, prepares for the church of tomorrow, always identical and yet rejuvenated and renewed.

We need to be together in this act of renewed faith because

we often find ourselves, both Catholics and Protestants, faced with the same questions and the same problems.

Some Christians seem to suffer from the fact that they are a minority in the world, as if Christ was not alone on the cross and as if the apostles were not only a handful in the pagan world. This feeling of being a minority gives to some an obsession with numbers, and we see a multitudinous concept of the church appear: they want many men to be Christians, even at the price of a devaluation of the faith, and they like to speak of "anonymous Christians" in order to persuade themselves that the church is assembling the multitude of men; basically, they are trying to save an outdated situation of Christianity. There is in this a constraint of human liberty which, while more spiritual than was the secular arm in the Middle Ages, is nonetheless still an obsession with numbers and unity at any price.

Christ did not promise us the conversion of the world such as it is, nor did he ask the Christian to make himself all things to all men to the degree that he think that finally a way to God can be found as well in the world as in the church, as well in human brotherhood as in the gospel.

Christ told us, "You are the salt of the earth; but if the salt loses its taste, with what can it be salted?" We are called not to be the earth, but to be the salt. And the taste of the salt which we are is faith. We will not find this taste in the earth, but in the salt; we will not discern Christ's message in the world, but in the gospel. If it is correct to think that we see Christ, too, working among men who do not believe, if we can discern his face in that of our non-Christian brother, it is because we have first of all contemplated him in the gospel which revealed his love to us.

Christians without flavor who minimize faith in order to make it acceptable sometimes resemble "rich men's sons" who are gorged and sated from childhood, not only with a comfortable Christianity, but with all the advantages of a consumer society. Would they have the same "philosophical" problems if they were not tired by their Christianized well-being?

Some want to invite us to a kind of mini-Christianity within the reach of every man which requires little with regard to faith or life but is so much more universal! What would this washed-out salt be, without taste and so mixed in with the world that there could be no helping it? In order to live, the earth requires that we be true salt. It is certainly necessary that we be possessed by a desire to proclaim the gospel all the way to the ends of the earth; and it is right that we feel disturbed by the dechristianization of the world. But it is not up to us to count the faithful of Christ, to number those whom he saves in his mercy beyond the limits of the church or to take a census of the People of God. What is demanded of the servants that we are is that we be found faithful. There is no fidelity for the Christian except in the full faith of the gospel. Our world cannot use a Christianity without the taste of faith; it needs true Christians who confess total faith, the salt of the earth, among the good pagans whose destiny God knows and whom he leads to his truth and salvation by secret ways which he alone can trace.

We feel a particular sympathy for the publican in the gospel, the ordinary man, plunged in the difficulties of life, at grips with the world and its temptations, who does not practice religion very much but who finds God in life and in communion with men. But Christ does not praise the publican's human situation, his moral indigence or his weak religious practice. Christ emphasizes his humility, his repentance and the absence of judgment in his heart; and it is this which is his justification; it is because of this that he returns home with a profound sentiment of God's pardon.

Likewise, Christ does not condemn the Pharisee for being a religious man, for leading a good moral life or for faithfully practicing his religion by fasting or paying tithes. He criticizes his spirit of judgment which makes him think that only his form of religious life can merit God's grace for him. It is only because he judges others that he returns home with less assurance of God's mercy and that he remains uneasy and troubled.

If Christ were to repeat the parable today for certain persons who flatter themselves with being just and who scorn others, perhaps he might change the roles and make the publicans of our times say, "My God, I thank you that I am not like these retarded Christians, who are too attached to the traditional faith, to the liturgy or to the morality of the church. I am a modern and free Christian. I pray sometimes, but I live fully integrated in our world where I meet Christ much better than in the churches . . ." We can be sure that in our inverted parable the modern publican would not go home justified.

Christ wants to tear us away from judging our brothers in the church. He is no more with the publicans than with the Pharisees; he is with the humble who repent and do not judge others.

There are people in our day who say that the Christian life has nothing to do with religion or with the traditional Christian attitudes which have constituted a great obstacle to Christianity's penetration into the world. They want to favor a Christian life without religious elements, consisting of nothing more than presence in the world. They think that Christ condemned traditional religion in the Pharisee, and that in the publican he recommended the non-religious world which can attain faith without traditional religious practice.

Christ condemned the spirit of judging one Christian attitude over another. Indeed, Christian faith is not to be confused with a religious attitude; but neither is it a-religious. It is above these human options. In its dynamism it carries along both the religious and the non-religious man, the Pharisee and the publican, the traditionalist and the modern, on condition that they do not judge one another and that they see their respective positions as complementary and not as hostile in the service of Christ.

There is also a third way in which the parable might have been written, in which the Pharisee and the publican thank God, one for the other, because they know that they are weak without each other and that they complement each other. Then, as different as they are, they both go home justified, at peace with God and with themselves, because Christ does not give peace according to our human options but according to the faith to which we are committed in humility, a humility that is the absence of judgment.

Human violence often takes possession of Christians in the present tensions at the heart of the church. Non-violence must be promoted, not only among all men, but also and primarily among Christians of diverse tendencies. How, indeed, can they proclaim the gospel of reconciliation and peace to men if they do not live it intensely among themselves? In this matter, Doctor Martin Luther King, a contemporary martyr for the gospel, reminded us that everything can be renewed in pardon:

> We should develop and maintain our aptitude for pardon. The man who is not capable of pardoning is not capable of loving. It is impossible for a man to begin only by loving his enemies, if he has not first of all accepted the necessity, unceasingly renewed, of pardoning those who inflict evil and injustice. Pardon is a catalyst which creates the necessary surroundings for a new start and a new beginning.

The World in the Church

The church is in dialogue with the world. Today, it judges the world very optimistically. This estimation of the world goes so far that some Christians are asking themselves what really distinguishes them from non-Christians and even from agnostics or atheists. Therefore, is the church on the point of dissolving itself in the world, and is the Christian, eager for human communion, disposed to be silent about the fact that he belongs to Christ because this distinguishes him too much from other men? The church is in the world, but the world is also in the church; how can they dialogue without confusion?

There is in the church and in the world a domain of God and a domain of temptation. The church, in the world and penetrated by the world, has a function of sanctifying, illuminating and discerning values of creation which are in the world and which, without the church, would become corrupted. The world, saved by the risen Christ, can remind the church of its universality and can lead it to broaden its heart ever increasingly to the dimensions of the universe.

The Christian is fully man. He cannot abstract himself from the world and become an angel. He lives in total solidarity with men and with the world. But, as a member of the Body of Christ, the church, transfigured by the word and the sacraments of Christ, he is a man-sign in the world. Fully man immersed in the world, the Christian is, in the discretion of love, a sign that the world is marching toward the fulfillment of God's reign.

The Christian, belonging simultaneously to the church and to the world, is an evangelical, baptismal, eucharistic and diaconal sign for men, his brothers. The Christian is an evangelical sign: Fully man and bound up with the world, he is also a man who wants to listen to the liberating word of the gospel in regard to every human situation. He wants, with the discretion of love, to benefit all men, his brothers, among whom he should witness to Christ and to Christ's truth and love. The Christian is a baptismal sign: A man like all others and plunged in the world, he is also a man marked with the sign of Christ which makes him a member of a community, the church. By this, he witnesses to the fact that man is no longer alone but is a member of God's family; and he is therefore close to every man to enable him to share in a life of brotherhood.

The Christian is a eucharistic sign: In full communion with man, his neighbor, and with all the aspirations of this world, he is also united to Christ, and primarily so by communion with his living and really present person. By the Eucharist he is transfigured to the image of Christ, the man-God, and he becomes ever increasingly the witness to an invisible presence of the first love which surpasses all human joy. But he knows that this communion which he realizes in a unique way in the Eucharist extends itself to his encounter with every man in whom he discerns God's image. In love for man and in service to man, it is still Christ who loves and serves.

The Christian is a diaconal sign: Near to every man and sharing in the sufferings of the world, he is the servant of all, ready to give himself to the human causes of justice and peace and ready to give his life for his friends, all men, according to Christ's example. In this sense, every Christian is a man of sacrifice; he is part of the royal and prophetic priesthood of Christ. If he has received a gift of ministry in the church, he is a servant of the priesthood of Christ and of all the church; he is ordained to augment, by means of the word and the sacraments, the priestly body of all his fellow Christians in the service of the world and of all men.

Thus, without being distinguished exteriorly from other men, the Christian, fully man, is the sign of a humanity transfigured by Christ and called to eternal life. He can share every human situation and every one of the world's aspirations with one exigency written in his heart, namely, that he do his best to make his fellowmen more human, that is, united to God whether they know it or not.

If the Christian, a man like others, and if the church, made of the dough of the world, can bring humanity this sign of Christ's presence without which it will die, the world, ransomed by Christ crucified and secretly brought along by its risen Lord, can also bring to the church and to the Christian a light which comes from God. If it is attentive to the history of men, sensitive to the signs of the times and anxious to listen to the entire world in its rich cultural diversity, the church becomes more universal and understands better all of the implications of the gospel which it bears in Christ's name.

Certainly, the world brings nothing but human values to the

church. It is also an arena where the powers of evil and sin seek constantly to take the upper hand. But it is not merely outside of itself that the church meets this world of sin; made of the world of men, the church also knows sin. Certainly, by the word, the sacraments and the ministry of Christ which it bears, the church is holy and is unceasingly sanctified; but the object of this sanctification is not only the sinners on the outside but also the sinners on the inside, Christians themselves.

Therefore, it is this rich and complex concept of the world, neither pessimistic nor too optimistic, which the church should make its own in order to dialogue better with the world in truth. In reality this dialogue is an interior one because the church finds the world within itself and because this world belongs to the Lord. The church is that part of the world which knows and announces Christ.

United in this way to the world by the very will of Christ, Lord of the church and of the world, the church cannot think of itself as a closed society, a pious ghetto, or a battle fortress. United to Christ as the Body of Christ, the church is united to him in the midst of the world, humanity and history. However, it is not in the midst of the world like a triumphant queen, but, according to Mary's example, like a humble servant, a servant of Christ and of men. As the center which radiates Christ's love, the church, in reality, has neither borders nor walls. It is defined according to its proper center, Christ crucified and risen, present in the church by word, sacraments and ministry; but it is not limited to borders more or less distant from this living center. It carries the rays of the sun of justice beyond the limits of the world; it is essentially universal: it recognizes as its own every man who is on his way towards God, every human culture, every race, every nation, every aspiration for the good and the beautiful, every discovery of science and every creation of art. It judges and rejects only evil and sin, injustice, war and death because these realities, in the world and in the church, have already been condemned by Christ the Lord.

The church, universal by nature, the friend of all men and the radiating center of the world without borders, the humble servant of Christ and of all humanity, tends constantly to a universal ecumenism. If it seeks its internal unity, the visible unity of all the baptized, it is not in order to be self-satisfied and to stop there. It wants to blend itself in with the universal brotherhood of all men in order to bring to them the only light and the only love which can save them, the light and love of the Father of the human family, of the First-born of all creation, of the vivifying Spirit who renews the face of the earth.

One day at the entrance to a city on the border between Galilee and Samaria, ten lepers cried out to Christ, "Jesus, Master, have pity on us!" Because of their sickness they were on the margin of society, kept at a distance by the people, cut off from the community. They constituted among themselves a kind of community of misery in which even a heretical Samaritan had his place among the orthodox Jews; in such misery what do confessional differences matter? It was a community of suffering, wandering in desert places, approaching no closer than the border of villages and signaling from a distance for the people to keep away. For us, sin, revolt, suffering and sadness also constitute a kind of leprosy which separates us from others. Then, we feel our solidarity with so many men who, like us, are tainted by sin and suffering. We are part of this community of weakness and misery without distinction of society or religion. If there is not yet eucharistic intercommunion between Christians, there is at least a real intercommunion of misery and weakness: we are all one in the presence of Christ whom we call upon from the distance of our common sin.

But why, out of ten lepers, did nine not return immediately to thank Christ? He had told them to go to the priest so that the latter could perform the rite of purification of lepers as set down by the law of Moses. On their way they could see that they were cured. Why didn't they all return?—we have to understand their situation. Having been so long on the margin of society, they were in a hurry to make themselves alright with the law, to return to a normal human situation after the ceremony of purification, to be reestablished in the community of men. The human fruits of the miracle of their healing preoccupied them more than the miracle itself, more than him who in his great mercy had cured them. Already they were accustomed to God's miracle, and they were ready to give it a human interpretation: after all, cures of leprosy have been seen before; it is not so extraordinary; perhaps it is the effect of medicine taken the night before? The essential thing now was to run to the priest who would restore everything to order and permit them to take up again their normal lives as men in the society of normal men.

We also, saved, regenerated, healed and consoled by Christ, are often more prompt to rejoice at the peace we have found or the well-being of a life without problems than we are to thank God for all of these blessings. We grow too accustomed to God's grace which has always transformed our lives and to all the blessings with which he showers us each day. We are tempted to forget that every peace and every joy is nourished by God's vivifying presence. We attribute to the happy events of our lives the joys which fill them and perhaps to our psychic equilibrium the peace in which we live. Healed with the great healing worked by baptism and the Eucharist, we want to be rid not only of leprosy, of the sin of revolt against God, but also of all the little evils in our existence which God asks us to bear until the time of his Kingdom.

Now we return to the tenth leper, the heretical Samaritan who did not know God like the orthodox Jews, but who knew enough to become our spiritual director with regard to detachment from the world in thanksgiving and contemplation. Instead of going first of all to straighten out his human situation by means of the priest's purification, he thinks only of him who cured him; he stops, returns on his tracks and thinks only of adoring and thanking his Savior. When we lose a sense of the supernatural in our lives and a taste for prayer of thanksgiving, we lose our faith little by little, like the nine lepers who re-entered healed into the community of men but without the imperishable joy of faith. Jesus said to the leper prostrate at his feet, "Rise up and go; your faith has saved you." It is faith in God's miracle in our lives which saves us. We should never treat as ordinary the extraordinary in a miracle or in faith which alone enables us to live each day in thanksgiving for the wonders of God.

Demand for Reinterpretation

Secularization is an invitation for the church to pursue its effort of hermeneutics, the translation of scriptural language into modern language, the passage of Christian truth from a past culture to contemporary culture, the transmission of God's word in a vocabulary which can be understood by the man of today.

The hermeneutical problem or, in other words, the interpretation and translation of Holy Scripture from one culture into another is one of the most important problems facing the church today. The problem of demythologizing is closely bound up with it. It is a matter of positive work on the part of the church with regard to the language of scripture and tradition, which is the necessary response to everything modern science and technology have called into question. If the first Christians had no difficulty in expressing the mystery of Christ's ascension, for example, by believing literally in their cosmological vocabulary when they said, "he ascended into heaven and sits at the right hand of the Father," it is quite evident that contemporary man cannot conceive of the cosmic heaven as the privileged place of the divine presence. Here we must be careful not to take our predecessors in the faith as being more literal or fundamentalist than they really were. Criticism of the material "beyond" or of the "three cosmic levels" (heaven, earth, hell), was made long before Robinson engaged in it. Some advocates of demythologizing would like to make us believe that our generation is the first to consider such problems. However, as Father Congar wrote in *Esprit* (October 1967):

With regard to "he sits at the right hand of the Father," for example, St. Thomas Aquinas and so many others with him have said that, applied to spiritual realities, what we express in spatial images, in terms of place, should be interpreted in terms of relation. These words of the Credo simply signify that Jesus received communication of the sovereign power of the Master of the world . . .

Calvin, likewise, opposed the partisans of a literal interpretation of Scripture:

These good doctors, to appear as learned men, forbid us to depart from the letter in any way at all. I reply that when Scripture calls God a man of war (Ex. 15:3), because this language without translation would be too hard and harsh, I do not fear to understand it as a comparison made with men. And in fact, the heretics who were called anthropomorphites in ancient times troubled the Church in no other way than in taking these words literally: the eyes of God see (Prov.

15:3), it came to His ears (Ps. 18 7), His hand is out-
stretched (Es. 9:11), the earth is His footstool (Es. 66:1);
they criticized the fact that the holy doctors did not agree that
God is corporal, despite the fact that all of Scripture assigns a
body to Him. They certainly had the letter on their side! But if
every passage were taken as crudely and heavily, all of the
true religion would be perverted to brutal dreams!

The Dutch Catechism says nothing completely new on this
subject, although it had reason to mention it when it affirms
with regard to the mystery of the ascension: "We must, therefore, leave aside our spatial representations. What we know is
that Jesus as man is with the Father . . . We do not know what
is the nature of this existence, which is the beginning of the new
creation."[5]

Even if the church has made a constant hermeneutical effort,
new problems will appear tomorrow, and Christians must be
spiritually and theologically armed to confront them without
fear of losing their faith and with discretion and humility. It is
not the more or less mythical images used by an ancient culture
to grasp God's word that are essential to the Christian faith; the
thing that is essential is this word itself, for which a vehicle
should be provided today by other representations belonging to
a world that can be believed in, namely, our modern world of
science and technology. The thing that constitutes God's revelation, that should be communicated to the man of today, is
not the words of Holy Scripture or of Christian tradition but
rather their meaning which can give birth to a new language.
The thing that is important and is already affirmed in the New
Testament is not the letter but the spirit. The letter can kill,

[5] *A New Catechism: Catholic Faith for Adults,* (New York, Herder &
Herder, 1967), p. 191.

whereas the spirit gives life. Rejection of the hermeneutical problem and of demythologizing can mean death.

If the Christianity of today and tomorrow should accept this translation of God's eternal and immutable revelation into a new language, it cannot do it by a new work of creation that starts from zero and cuts itself off from the continuous tradition which binds it to the faith of the apostles and Fathers of the church. Only the church, as the community in which the Spirit lives, founded on the faith of the apostles, the body of Christ, can proceed to this renewal of language, to this "transculturization" of the gospel, to this passage of revelation into the contemporary world. Certainly scholars, exegetes and theologians have an important role in the search for solutions to the problems posed; but it belongs to all the People of God to confess the Christian faith in a language of today, leaving aside its outdated and useless wrappings and faithfully keeping the good deposit without which there would be no more church or Christianity. Here, the church, as the People of God led by its ministers, has an indispensable role; and this role should itself be made an object of research. To be sure, the theologian knows that his science is not an individual exercise and that it is not merely the work of a team, but that the Spirit who dialogues with the church should furnish it with the elements indispensable to its historical or philosophical research. This theological role of every church is exercised through its liturgical prayer, its contemplation, the witness of each one of its members and through the combat and suffering of its faithful.

The church can discover today and tomorrow the new language of God's revelation only if it truly remains the apostolic church, founded on the faith of the apostles. Christ did not write, but he gave a mandate to the apostles to transmit the gospel all the way to the ends of the earth. After Christ's resurrection through the gift of the Holy Spirit, the apostles understood the history of Jesus in all its depth; they had a paschal and pentecostal understanding of it. Then, since they belonged to the Christian community which was living in intimacy with the risen Savior by means of prayer and the sacraments, they also received from the church a deepening of their understanding of what they had experienced with Christ and heard from him. Thanks to the light of the resurrection and to the Holy Spirit in them and in the church, the apostles understood better and more deeply the life and words of Christ, whose humanity had often veiled his divinity from them during the course of his earthly life. They plumbed the mystery of the Incarnation in all of its depth. When they transmitted and then wrote the history and words of Christ, they did not do it like journalists or historians, but in an act of contemplation and catechesis. Even if they developed the literalness of this history and these words, their narrations are truer than if the events had been registered by means of modern techniques. What God wanted to transmit through Christ was not limited to events and words; it was a profound mystery of life and meaning which could be attained only after Christ's resurrection with the illumination of the Spirit and the contemplative and sacramental life of the church, the community of intimacy with the living and present Christ.

For the apostles and the New Testament writers, the profound meaning of the evangelical revelation surpassed material facts and the mere literal meaning of words. For us also, as for the apostolic church, what is infinitely more important than an anecdotal detail in Jesus' life is the theological and spiritual meaning which we discern beneath the words by means of the overwhelming light of the Resurrected and of the Spirit. This life can be experienced in prayer and in the existence of the

Christian community intimately united to its Lord, today, yesterday and always.

In order to communicate God's word today, we need not fear if certain images, expressions, myths or words belonging to a world in the past dwindle or disappear. What interests us fundamentally is that the eternal and immutable word of God, transmitted first of all by the apostles and then many times in the tradition of the church, passes today in all its intensity of saving truth to the heart of contemporary man with his ways of thinking and feeling conditioned by science and technology.

In this new understanding of the gospel, just as for the apostles, the living and praying ecclesial community has a capital role. As for them, the church which lives with the Resurrected and dialogues with the Spirit is a necessary and indispensable place for an understanding in depth of the word of God deposited in scripture. With the actual effort of hermeneutics, the translation of the language of Christian truth, an effort to understand the relations between scripture and the living tradition of the church must be pursued. Indeed, without this understanding of the role of the church, the body of the risen Christ and the spouse of the Holy Spirit, on the level of hermeneutical research, the latter runs the danger of being no more than the individualistic enterprise of a few scholarly exegetes who will call the foundations of the faith into question without being able to build them up again. Conversely, integration into the contemplation and life of the church offers to the hermeneutical effort a chance to really attain its scientific goal, since Christian truth, before being thought, is first of all lived in union with him who is the Truth, Christ risen and living in the church.

The Permanence of Contemplation

Although the problems of secularization and hermeneutics will increasingly come to the forefront among the church's preoccupations, the problem of prayer, both liturgical and personal, is undeniably just as important. In a world where technology foresees the solution to many of man's problems posed by nature and history, in a consumer society like ours where everything is within reach of the hand and the pocketbook, it is sometimes difficult for contemporary man to position the role and the necessity of prayer. Man in the Middle Ages or during the Reform lived much more in a feeling of powerlessness in relation to the forces of nature and in a much greater poverty with regard to the riches of the earth. He found in prayer a compensation for his weakness and a recourse to God on whom he had to count at every instant in order to survive. The discoveries of the human mind and easier satisfaction for the needs of the body have called into question the necessity of a prayer of total dependence and of constant request. But this new problem of prayer, far from turning us away from prayer as useless, can lead us today and tomorrow to a deeper understanding of its vital meaning.

Prayer appears much more today to be an effort of conscious communication with God. It is not primarily a request that God shower us with our material needs; rather, and more deeply, it is a contemplation of Christ so that he give us the dispositions to collaborate with him for the good of the world.

People today sometimes think that prayer runs the danger of cutting the Christian off from his solidarity with men, that it places him in a privileged ivory tower and that it alienates his true human nature. These people want a Christianity without prayer, sometimes even one without God, so that it be more completely integrated into the ordinary existence of the world. But we know very well deep in our Christian consciousness that the Christianity of tomorrow, like the Christianity of yesterday, cannot subsist as such without prayer. One thing we must do, however, is to consider how our prayer should evolve in order to correspond with our situation as modern men.

Prayer should be increasingly integrated into life; it should be part of daily life. The world's agitation and the resulting difficulty for spiritual concentration no longer permit us to set aside long moments of meditation and prayer. Some persons have, perhaps, been able to conserve this grace, but it cannot be made the rule for the man of today. New ways have to be found for contemplative prayer which will penetrate all of one's existence. It is good to find a moment, a quarter of an hour let us say, to read the Bible and to place ourselves in Christ's presence, offering ourselves to collaborate with him in the world and presenting to the light of his grace the names of those who are confided to us; but we must find simple ways to make a sentiment of God's presence rise to our consciousness at every moment of the day, at work, at our meals and while we are resting. Here the old practice of Jewish benedictions can be of help. Bless God for everything lived in his presence and in his communion. This constant prayer, or rather this spirit of prayer penetrating all of our life, is truly proper to the Christian life: "Pray without ceasing," wrote St. Paul. He did not mean by this that we must continually draw aside and get on our knees to make a vocal and elaborate intercession. Formed in Jewish piety, he rather wanted to invite the Christian to a contemplative benediction or thanksgiving for everything and for every man encountered during the different moments of the day. This unceasing prayer to Christ, recognized in every man encountered, is truly proper to the Christian life of prayer. The oriental spirituals, with their practice called the "prayer of Jesus," have found in their own way this simple, fundamental, contemplative prayer which our modern faith needs for tomorrow: "Lord Jesus, have mercy on me . . . have mercy on him . . . may you be blessed for the water . . . for the sun . . . for our food . . . for science . . . for technology . . . for television . . . for rapid communications . . . for the atomic discoveries used for peaceful purposes . . ."

If personal prayer is called into question, the church's liturgical prayer poses an even greater problem today. Many think that the Catholic Mass is too characterized by the sacrificial spirit of the Middle Ages and that Protestant cult is too marked by the intellectualistic teaching of the sixteenth century Reformers. They consider as outdated the priest who offers a sacrifice for the people and the pastor who preaches a word too often repeated to tired ears, to hearts that are thirsty for something concrete. They want a cult that is more human, more simple, more of the present. Certainly, the liturgical reform which is taking place, more resolutely in the Catholic Church than in those of the Reform, will aid the evolution of a Christian worship which will better correspond with the mentality of the man of tomorrow.

At this stage we must make a few reservations. The liturgy of the church, the act of the People of God, is not a fabricated thing. It is part of the church's tradition of contemplative experience. If cult were no more than the actual expression of the religious sentiments of contemporary man, it would not be formative of faith and prayer. There is an objectivity in the liturgy necessary for a pedagogy of faith. Cult forms our minds and our hearts according to the light of the secular experience of the church which has lived on God's word and on the sacraments of his presence. Therefore, there is always a traditional aspect in the liturgy, something which comes to us from the past and which inserts us into a tradition of prayer which goes back to the apostles. The liturgy must surpass us in order to enable us to surpass ourselves; it must disengage us from the preoccupations of the world in order to engage us better in the world with that light of Christ which it makes shine in us, with that fire of love which it enkindles in our hearts. As Paul Ricoeur has said, we must accept being "progressive in politics and archaic in poetry," we must conclude "a new pact between technology and poetry." We can transpose this as follows: If the church should be progressive in its missionary attitude with regard to the world, it should be conservative in its liturgical attitude before God. However, conserving the essential does not mean conserving everything just because it is clothed with the prestige of antiquity. The liturgy is not archeology; it is the continuity of the prayer of the People of God who draw out from their treasure "nova et vetera," the new and the traditional. The worship of tomorrow should not be to our measure, but to the measure of God's word and the church's continuous prayer, which should form our faith, inform our love and con-from us to the life of Christ crucified and risen.

Today people want to take the sacredness out of Christian life and to remove from it every religious or mystical characteristic. Following their poor understanding of Bonhoeffer, they want a "Christianity without religion," that is, without liturgy, without mystery, without prayer. Intellectual and moral Christianity, life according to a gospel stripped of all contemplation, an existence of generosity without God: don't the Marxists do as much? Christianity can remain the Christian faith only if it is lived as an obedience to the God of Jesus Christ, a personal and transcendent God, who calls us to faith, hope, love, prayer, contemplation and thanksgiving in communion with a church assembled in his name to serve him and to serve the world.

The cult of the church, which culminates in the holy supper, the Eucharist, brings us into communion with a mystery which cannot be explained but only lived in a contemplative attitude. In this communion with the mystery of Christ's living presence man descends to the depths of his own mystery, he attains the deepest part of his being, he touches the sacred in his life and destiny. It is false to think that modern man no longer has a sense of the sacred. Although he willingly does without God and the church, he reconstitutes feast days and liturgies in which he can rediscover the proximity of the mystery of his existence. There comes immediately to mind here the celebrations of the communities of "hippies" who go so far as to seek in drugs the contemplation of the great voyage to the depths. When man no longer wants the mystery of God, he finds feasts and liturgies which plunge him into his own mystery, when it is not into the mystery of the powers of darkness . . .

The liturgy of tomorrow will be simpler and more human, but the authenticity of its language and the actuality of its forms should be inserted into the continuity of the prayer of the church. We may celebrate the holy supper in people's homes with less solemnity than in our cathedrals of today, but the Eucharist must remain the same Eucharist which all the generations of Christians have lived, the sacrament of Christ's presence, celebrated with fervor as the mystery of the living God nourishing the faithful; it cannot be merely a fraternal agape. The liturgical reading of the Bible can never be replaced by the reading of a newspaper, even though the latter may seem to furnish greater relevance for the church's intercession. The liturgy is the employment of the word of God and of the sacraments of Christ, received in the continuity of the prayer of the church. As such, it is not only the expression of man's heart but the conformity of this heart to Christ's love which transcends all of our human sentiments.

We misunderstand the intent of the liturgical reform if we see in it nothing but novelty or simplification. It is rather a matter of a very healthy balance between a happy return to the biblical, patristic and liturgical sources and a truly pastoral responsibility. The present liturgical reform appears to be profoundly traditional; it emphasizes the fact that the church's liturgy, in order to be living and efficacious, must express the continuous experience of the common prayer of the People of God in its fundamental and proven forms. From this viewpoint, evidently, nothing is simultaneously more traditional and relevant than biblical prayer, that of the Fathers of the church, that of the golden age of the liturgy which covers the first five centuries of Christian history. The present liturgical reform does not cede to the temptation of archeology and does not want to resurrect ancient forms; but it recognizes the permanent value of the church's primitive experience and the living actuality of this first contact of the Christian people with God the Trinity, with Christ, true God and true man, adored and received by his ecclesial body in his word and in his sacraments.

We cannot emphasize sufficiently the ecumenical consequences of this return to the sources of the life and actuality of liturgical prayer. This universal liturgical reform is one of the most precious efforts being made towards the visible unity of all Christians. "Lex orandi, lex credendi": liturgical prayer fashions our faith. To the degree that we approach each other in the liturgy, we approach each other also in faith.

In their desire for a real presence in the world, some Christians willingly speak today of doing away with the sacred or of a Christianity without religious elements; they want to take the sacred out of the liturgy. But presence in the world, in order to be true, must be a Christian presence, that is, a presence of faith truly in the world and including all of its complexity and richness. The liturgy is precisely the most appropriate place for the renewal of faith which must then be brought into the world. Besides, the world, as is well known, reveals unsuspected attachments to religious sentiment and to the sacred. Is man so insensitive to the spirit of a celebration, for example? We could mention many cases where men want to celebrate a family or public event by means of a holiday that transports them outside of themselves and unites them profoundly to the human community. The true liturgy, renewed in its profound sources, is a celebration of the Christian community which surpasses itself in the sentiment of God's transcendent presence. The present liturgical reform enables us to rediscover this spirit of celebration, and it favors a new contact with this longing for celebration so rooted in the heart of man. The spirit of celebration is an essential aspect of the liturgy which usually demands a prepared place, vestments, singing, etc. The Eucharist itself, as the liturgy of a meal with Christ, is deeply in accord with the aspirations of man whose celebrations always culminate in a fraternal and joyful banquet. The extraction of the sacred is a false problem because man needs celebration, and celebration always has a sacred character. It is not necessary to take the sacred out of the liturgy; rather, all of its dimension as a communal celebration in God's presence must be found. Then, the liturgy will be for man a sign of Christ's presence as a friend who dialogues with the Christian community and has the meal of Emmaüs with it, the Eucharist, the banquet of the Kingdom.

The liturgical reform rediscovers this essential festive reality in man. Renewed in a biblical liturgy that is traditional and vital, the church prepares in prayer the visible unity of all Christians; and this unity will not be an easy compromise by taking the sacred out of Christianity nor a return to archaic forms that date from the ages of divisions. Rather, it will be a mutual rediscovery of separated brethren in the authenticity of prayer such as Christ lived it in the midst of his disciples and such as the primitive church experienced fundamentally. Then we will be able to share without restriction the celebration of our reconciliation in a common liturgy which will culminate in one same Eucharist.

The Eucharist as such, the mystery of the real presence of the Lord who gives himself, was never an ordinary meal. Christ instituted it in the context of a paschal meal, which was for the Jews a true liturgy in which Israel's historical deliverance was made present and in which God showered his people with the blessings of this unique liberation. Likewise, in the Eucharist we receive Christ really present with all the blessings derived from the sacrifice of his crucifixion and the glory of his resurrection for our lives as men. The Eucharist is a liturgical meal in which Christ himself offers us his Body and Blood under the signs of bread and wine.

In primitive Christianity, this Eucharist was sometimes celebrated on the occasion of a fraternal meal, an agape. But the

Eucharist was never confused with the agape. We even find St. Paul opposing any such confusion when he wrote to the Corinthians. The agape could again have its role in the church as a fraternal meal uniting men and women in a sharing of joy and suffering around a single table. This meal might be the occasion for divided Christians, Catholics, Orthodox and Protestants, to find themselves together again in sharing a common earthly food while waiting to be able to share the Eucharist in one same fundamental faith. This meal would be an occasion to pray together and to read the word of God and then to rejoice in common for the great part of Christian faith which they already share.

To remain in the truth, it is necessary to distinguish in this way the Eucharist, the liturgy in which Christ really present gives himself as a supernatural food, from the meal of the agape, a fraternal meeting where men eat earthly food together as a sign of the friendship of Christ which unites them. But, having said this, we can recall that the primitive church also wanted to retain for the Eucharist its character as a meal, even though it is a liturgical meal, a mystery, a sacrament, so true is it that in Christ, man-God, everything human finds its place to be consecrated to God.

In the Eucharist we clearly see Christ's deliberate will to integrate into the Christian community the constitutive elements of a human community: a meal, dialogue, service, a sharing of the joys and difficulties of existence. The description of the first Christian community in the Acts of the Apostles (2:42-47) gives these same constitutive elements of the human community as constitutive of the community united around the risen Christ in the power of the Spirit: Christ's community, which has only one heart and one soul, is united by the breaking of bread (Eucharist) or by the fraternal meal (agape); it is assiduous in following the teaching of the apostles, and it expresses its praise; it encourages the sharing of goods for the service of all; it cries out its joy and includes the cares of men in its intercessory prayer. Today, the fraternal community is better realized either in little friendly groups or among larger crowds of people. The Eucharist, also, must be adaptable to these two forms: in small groups or in large assemblies in basilicas or in the open air (pilgrimages, celebrations, etc.)

The forms of eucharistic celebration should be signs of a meal. Evidently, the Eucharist is a liturgical (paschal) meal, not an ordinary meal. However, the elements of which it is composed should be fully authentic. On the other hand, the rediscovery of the agape should provide a fraternal and ecumenical complement to the Eucharist, which at present cannot always be the actual sign of unity in the divided church and the post-Christian world.

Modern man does not accept very well a paternalistic discourse under the form of a monologue; he wants to be able to react with questions and dialogue. The time for concentration which our contemporaries have is very limited. This fact calls upon us to make a readjustment of the forms of preaching. The sharing of goods, mutual aid, the question of money, these should rediscover their close bond with the liturgy; modern man does not accept social inequality which contradicts the community of worship. The Eucharist expresses the church's overflowing and missionary joy; here, the forms of joy and ecstasy which young people have in song should have access to the liturgy, passing through the transfiguration of the adoration of Christ in the purity of the Spirit. Intercessory prayer should express a true sharing in human suffering; it is closely bound up with service. We cannot pray for men in difficulty without wanting to help them and without fulfilling this desire.

The Eucharist, the true liturgy of communion with Christ's real presence, can also be a true human celebration in which the legitimate aspirations of the man of today find their accomplishment in the transfiguration worked by Christ.

The Eucharist is not an act of remembering Christ subjectively but of proclaiming his presence, death and resurrection objectively. It is not an act in memory of Christ but an objective memorial, the very presence of Christ crucified and risen which the church celebrates in thanksgiving and prayer. By the memorial of the Eucharist, Christ's death and resurrection become present to the church; Christians become their contemporaries. This is what St. Paul means when he affirms, "As often as you eat this bread and drink the cup, you proclaim the Lord's death until he comes" (I Cor. 11:26).[6] It is not a matter of remembering or of recalling to memory a past event; it is a matter of proclaiming the presence and accomplishing the memorial of Christ crucified and risen, living always to intercede for us.

But there is still more in the memorial of the Eucharist. In the time of Jesus, the memorial expressed a sacrifice presented to God as a thanksgiving and supplication so that he might remember his faithful and shower them with his blessings. The Eucharist is also a memorial presented to the Father as a thanksgiving and supplication. The church presents the memorial of the Eucharist to the Father to thank him and to petition him in the name of Christ dead and risen. The word memorial underlines the Eucharist's sacrificial character. The memorial of the Lord is therefore the proclamation of the victory of the cross in the world and the presentation to the Father of the unique sacrifice of Christ as the praise and intercessory prayer of the church.

[6] *The Holy Bible, Revised Standard Version* (New York, Nelson, 1953). Copyright 1946 and 1952 by the Division of Christian Education of the National Council of the Churches of Christ in the U.S.A.

Simplifying the Institution

The secularization of the world places the institution of the church in a critical situation. In a culture determined by Christianity, the church could rest on numerous institutional forms which were not called into question. It could maintain confessional schools and hospitals directed by religious communities; the bishop had his place among the civil authorities, the priest or the pastor was the spiritual leader of the village; feast days and liturgies marked the daily life of the people; Sunday was respected by everyone as a day of rest. This situation, which we are describing quickly in a past tense, is still present in some places to a considerable degree. But everything leads us to think that the future will bring radical criticism of this type of interpenetration of Christianity and the world. Some people within the church itself, especially young persons who have a presentiment of the future, are severely critical of the church as an institution. There certainly is a little confusion in this criticism between institution and organization. Some say that they are against the institution of the church because they can no longer see, for example, the grounds for parochial organization. This needs a little clarification.

The church, which is fundamentally a communion, a community of men who believe in and confess Christ, God and Savior, necessarily takes its place in the world where it cannot help but appear as an organized society. From being a spiritual communion the church continually becomes a social institution to the extent that it must necessarily organize to live and endure in the world. The church is always simultaneously communion and institution, community and society. The vocabulary of construction employed by the New Testament to designate the development of the Church ("I will build my church," Christ said.) implies an institutional concept of the church since its apostolic foundation.

But the secularization of the world, the fact that men can do without God and that human society is disengaging itself more and more from domination by Christianity, all this questions the institution of the church in the multiple forms of organization which it has assumed during the course of centuries. Large sections of its walls have cracked and are threatening to crumble. In face of this threatening destruction, the church must now know how to discern what is fundamental in its structure as an institution from what is merely accidental and due to outdated historical situations in which it formerly and legitimately took its place.

The church must reflect lucidly on what is absolutely specific and necessary to its existence in order to learn how to rid itself easily and without regret of institutions that were instruments of its life and mission in the past, but which are in danger of being swept away in the future. If the church clings in a reactionary attitude to these institutions which are really not essential to it, they could even constitute a troublesome handicap to its witness in the contemporary world.

This time of crisis and of criticism of institutions is also a time of research into specific questions. What is it that makes the church the church wanted by Christ, both as communion and institution? What makes the Christian a Christian, different from other men as well as one among them? What is it that makes the minister, pastor or priest, different by his vocation from other members of the People of God, not to dominate them as children but to serve them as adult collaborators? What constitutes the specificity of Christians, men or women, who are committed to a life of prayer and service at the heart of a community which includes remaining celibate?

The church is, at the heart of the People of God who overflow it, a sign or sacrament of Christ's presence, word and work in the world. Tomorrow it will remain this as it was yesterday. Without becoming a closed ghetto or a battle fortress, the church cannot allow itself to be confused with the world that surrounds it. It is that part of humanity which confesses Jesus Christ as God and Savior. To be this discernible and undiluted sign in the world, it should proclaim God's word contained in Holy Scripture which is its first institutional form. There is an institution of scripture which the church can never renounce without betraying its mission, even though, as we have seen, its exegesis must continually be brought up to date. The sign of the church is also manifested by its sacramental institution. By means of baptism it brings members of the People of God into its visible communion and it constitutes them a missionary community to render a living witness to Christ. By means of the Eucharist, which implies the proclamation of the word of God and the meal of the Lord really present, the church continually assembles the Christian community to nourish its faith, hope, charity and prayer with a view to its living presence in the world.

By means of the various ordained ministries, the church organizes the faithful into unity and charity with a view to mutual service and the service of all men. The institution of the church, necessary to its communion and its mission, is essentially scriptural, sacramental and ministerial. Outside of these three specific forms of the ecclesial institution the other institutional aspects of the church are only accidental, due to historical situations and, therefore, temporary. The church could very well, in the future, present itself under the form of little communities corresponding more to the human level than do parishes, communities defined by a house, street or section. Here the word of God would be studied fraternally during evenings spent with each other; baptism would be celebrated by a diaconal minister and the Eucharist celebrated in the homes by an ordained minister who has not necessarily specialized in university studies. The churches could remain the context of the great liturgies of the People of God assembled on Sundays and on feast days; they could constitute zones of silence amid the noise of the modern city, be at the disposition of every man and be places of continuous music offered to the non-believer as to the Christian. We have to find a non-liturgical and non-Christian use for these great edifices which we can no longer keep for ourselves alone.

The institution of the church, brought back in this way to its necessary specificity, would allow a better insertion of the Christian community into the human community. The future will demand of the church that it be much more humanly present in the world, not as a great, powerful and very distinct society, but as the communion of authentic communities of men who know each other and help each other in their service to others and in their witness to the gospel of Christ. Such men would be at the heart of a living dialogue with contemporary man.

What is this specific witness of the Christian in the world of tomorrow? Quite evidently it remains penetrated with all of the gospel's message, understood in the light of the hermeneutical translation which makes God's eternal and immutable word burst forth in a language renewed by modern science and technology. For the Christian of today and tomorrow this integral message is dominated by an eschatological sense which makes him await the renewal of all creation by the presence and coming of the risen Christ and which commands detachment, asceticism and poverty with regard to the world such as it is. The non-Christian can live the moral consequences of the gospel in a certain spirit of charity, generosity and even sacrifice, but he does not know Christ's love and the ardent waiting for his presence and coming. The Christian is distinguished not by his moral virtues or his metaphysical intelligence, but by his friendship with the risen Christ, living and present, the Christ who comes to change the world and to make a new earth.

The Christian is essentially a man of faith, that is, a man who gives a sense of God to a world of the absurd. He is a man of hope, that is, a man who gives the perspective of Christ to a world of programs. He is a man of generous and self-sacrificing love, that is, a man who shares in a world of possessions. He is a man of contemplation, that is, a man whose vision goes beyond appearances to attain the profound mystery of the other and of the Spirit who wants to live in the hearts of men. With this faith, hope, love and contemplation the Christian is and will be a man like others, really integrated into the ordinary life of each one. He will be a sign of Christ's presence in the midst of the world, a question for the man who is satisfied with his humanity, a possible answer for the man who is searching for the sense of a life that is apparently without meaning.

Among other problems which agitate the internal life of the church there is one which we must mention because a new solution to it must be found tomorrow in continuity with the gospel and tradition; this is the problem of the ordained ministry in the church, of the priest or of the pastor. Many other aspects of the life of the church depend on the solution to this problem. In the critical updating of the institution of the church, what is the specificity of the ministry in the midst of the People of God? The pastor of tomorrow can no longer be the kind with which we are acquainted; and yet his fundamental identity must subsist since his ministry goes all the way back to that of the apostles of Christ. We certainly cannot foresee what will be determined by many factors that now escape us, but we can indicate a few perspectives on the basis of today's critical questions.

Tomorrow, as today, the ordained minister will be essentially a member of the People of God chosen by vocation to exercise the charge and service of the word, the sacraments and authority. He has the responsibility of forming the faith of Christians by the doctrine of the gospel, of sanctifying their lives by the celebration of the sacraments and of building up their community in charity and unity. Without these specific functions the ministry would not exist in the apostolic continuity of the church faithful to the gospel. However, the social form of the ministry will certainly change in the future.

Pastors are often cut off from the laity. We can ask ourselves whether their intellectual, seminary education does not clericalize them in a way that removes them from the laymen's ways of feeling the realities of this world. In the primitive church, pres-

byters were designated by reason of their ecclesial experience
and their capacity to transmit the word of God. They were
servants of the royal priesthood of the laymen and not a theological oligarchy.

To again obtain true contact between pastors and laymen, it
may well be necessary that in the future the majority of the
church's ministers have an ordinary job by which they can earn
enough to pay their personal expenses in keeping with the majority of men. Indeed, the truest contact with humanity takes
place at work. The society of the future will not accept as men
persons who do not participate in the common creation by
means of their work. Certainly, we believe that the ministry is a
creative work and very much so! But we cannot impose this
certitude on a secularized society. Since leisure time is increasing continually, the pastor, worker, employee, farmer, writer
and professor will also have time to accomplish a ministry, a
more restricted but more concentrated and efficacious one.
This implies an increase in the number of ministers, pastors
and deacons, an extension of ordination to a greater number of
laymen. Their biblical and theological formation will have to
be shorter, concentrated more on what is essential, and less
intellectualistic so as to avoid an evil clericalization which
would cut them off from the rest of the People of God.

Pope Paul VI reaffirmed the necessary bond in the Latin
Church between the priesthood and celibacy. Certainly, this
affirmation maintains a problem in the ecumenical dialogue;
but the doctrinal and pastoral exigencies of the Roman Catholic Church do not always allow it the openness which non-
Catholics demand in relation to unity. Whatever the reservations which non-Catholics make concerning this necessary
bond between the priesthood and celibacy, we must recognize
the theological and spiritual depth of this stance even in what

concerns the doctrine of celibacy consecrated to Christ. We can undersand equally the pope's pastoral anxiety concerning the celibacy of priests.

The text of Paul VI's encyclical shows first of all a great historical honesty in what concerns both the testimony of the New Testament and the writings of the Fathers. It also recalls the legitimate Oriental discipline which permits the priesthood of married men. The pope also manifests a great understanding of the problems facing celibate priests in the contemporary world. He does not conceal the ecumenical difficulties. Our point here is that this new affirmation of the bond between the priesthood and celibacy is situated in a context of pastoral and spiritual authenticity.

The monastic renewal in the churches which issued from the Reform has also prompted fresh reflection on the subject of celibacy, and it is striking to see the proximity of their points-of-view to certain of the fundamental affirmations of the encyclical. Protestants have much to learn from the evangelical doctrine expressed there in order to grasp still better that Christ calls certain ones in the church to remain celibate for his name's sake, for the gospel and for the Kingdom of God.

The first thing that stands out in the encyclical is that it views celibacy both as a charism, a gift of the Holy Spirit, and as a discipline. It belongs to the church to discern this "charism of consecrated celibacy." Celibacy is a gift of God for the service of the gospel and the church. Consecrated celibacy, a gift of God, is the object of a vocation for some, just as marriage is for others, amid the People of God.

The doctrinal part of the encyclical is certainly the most profound and the richest part and quite adequate to renew the evangelical sense of their vocation in all those who have received the gift of consecrated celibacy. It assigns three major significations to celibacy: Christological, ecclesiological and eschatological. According to its Christological signification, consecrated celibacy is a gift to Christ. It underlines the newness of the order of redemption in relation to the order of creation. It constitutes a call to love for Christ who alone can fully reply to the expectation of the person who gives himself fully to him. According to its ecclesiological signification, consecrated celibacy is a service to the church: a service to the word, the sacraments, prayer and the community of the faithful. Celibacy should invite devotion and generosity to the service of the church, according to the example of Christ who sacrificed himself totally for love of the church, his spouse. According to its eschatological signification, consecrated celibacy is a call to the Kingdom of God. It is a sign that the figure of this world is passing and that the People of God should march unceasingly towards its accomplishment, the Kingdom of the risen.

This doctrine of celibacy, which is so biblical, is quite adequate to renew in their distinct vocations both those who are consecrated to God in marriage and those who are consecrated to him in celibacy. More than ever, the church has urgent need for holiness by the sanctification of each Christian. Each unfaithfulness weakens the proclamation of the gospel and the radiance of the church. We have stressed very much during these last decades the church's qualities of unity, catholicity and apostolicity. Holiness also is a fundamental quality of the People of God and should be emphasized like the others. It even has a very particular role to play with regard to unity. Ecumenism is not only an effort to reunify ecclesial institutions; it is also an effort to sanctify all the members of the Body of Christ in a holy, spiritual emulation. The more we are near to Christ in sanctification, the more we will be near to each other. It is necessary for us to hear this call to sanctification and sacrifice for love of Christ and service to the church: the sanctification and sacrifice of some in consecrated celibacy, the sanctification and sacrifice of others in consecrated marriage. The greatest danger for Christians today is not the crisis of faith but forgetfulness of sanctification and the refusal of sacrifice. If it is to end up in unity, ecumenism also requires this sanctification and sacrifice in faithfulness to the vocation of Christ and to the gift of the Spirit, received by each one for the service of all.

It is indispensable that the church accomplish its updating today, its aggiornamento, by disengaging the specificity of the various aspects of its ministry, for fear that tomorrow, when the secularization of the world will put it still more into question, it may run the danger of abandoning, along with superfluous institutional wrappings, structures fundamental to its very being: ecclesial communion and the scriptural, sacramental and ministerial institution willed by Christ.

This aggiornamento should be a fact of all the churches. Today ecumenism takes the form of mutual help between churches in a healthy theological and spiritual emulation which favors their updating and at the same time encourages their visible unity better than did the dialogues in the recent past. Because the churches find themselves faced with the same problems of secularization and of criticism by the world, they are brought ever closer together in a same research for the language which will translate for the man of today the eternal word of God; they are encouraged to one same prayer; and they are invited to the same institutional purification. In this purificatory crisis, their same concept of unity will find itself enriched and deepened.

Unity among Sister-Churches

In the beginnings of ecumenism, unity was envisaged as an ideal, like Eden, lived by the primitive church, then lost, now to be refound in the more or less distant future. This unity was seen as the unification of the different pieces of Christianity, divided into churches, into one single, visible church. It was a concept of unity which stressed unification and uniformity (although mention was always made of healthy diversities) unconsciously influenced by western centralization.

Exegetical studies on the ecclesiology of the New Testament have shown that even while the apostles were living, there were diverse forms of churches coexisting in the fundamental unity maintained by the apostolic ministry. At Corinth we see a charismatic church whose only bishop seems to be the Holy Spirit who distributes his gifts and ministries in the community totally given over to his inspiration. To be sure, St. Paul's first epistle addressed to the Corinthians does not justify all the aspects of this ecclesial life, but it does not question it as totally erroneous. The Acts of the Apostles show us a church which certainly is also led by the Spirit but structured with a collegial presbyteral ministry. Then, the epistles to Timothy and Titus give us a view of churches directed by various hierarchical ministries and organized by the collaborator or successor of an apostle: it is already an outline of the episcopal system which the letters of St. Ignatius of Antioch, at the beginning of the second century, were to recognize as the ideal government of the church. We can consider this evolution from the purely charismatic church to the episcopal church as willed by God since it was never questioned until the time of the Reform except by very small evangelical groups. However, if the New Testament presents us with this ecclesiological pluralism, why, in the march towards unity which will probably be of an episcopal nature, can we not accept each other in the diversity of our ecclesial situations?

However, Vatican II called in question the tendency to uniformity in Roman centralization in favor of a rebirth of the concept of local churches, united to each other by episcopal collegiality, in the midst of which the primacy of the bishop of Rome is situated. This evolution in Roman ecclesiology frees ecumenism from its obsession with unification.

Then, during the visit of the pope to Constantinople and the visit of the Patriarch Athenagoras to Rome, both spoke of their churches as sister-churches. Catholicism and Orthodoxy seem to be orienting themselves toward a union between sister-churches which would be consecrated by intercommunion in a theological, dogmatic and liturgical diversity compatible with a more living and more real unity than pure and simple return to Roman unity. Isn't this the unity which the church of the first centuries knew: a fundamental unity in biblical faith, baptism and the Eucharist amid a great local diversity in the manifestations of the church and even of the ministry?

The encounters at Constantinople and at Rome between Pope Paul VI and the Patriarch Athenagoras I, the gesture of reconciliation which they made and the words of brotherhood which they exchanged constitute an event of important consequences for the theology of unity.

First of all, the evangelical environment of these encounters should be underlined. At Jerusalem the Pope and the Patriarch met each other outside of their own homelands but in their common spiritual homeland, the homeland of Christ. According to human protocol, the second encounter should have taken place at Rome and the third at Constantinople. This is what the Patriarch Athenagoras wanted; but we know the difficulties of every kind which then opposed it. And behold, human protocol was overturned by the protocol of the gospel, which is service and humility. The Pope, the first patriarch according to both Catholic and Orthodox traditions, went to the second patriarch, the Archbishop Athenagoras. Power became service, and prerogative became humility. How can this evangelical spirit not bring forth profound and solid fruits of unity? It is the high spiritual quality of this first encounter which enabled the second one at Rome to take place.

There is also a theological meaning to these gestures and to the words which made them explicit. Visible unity no longer appears under the form of a return of the Orthodox Church to obedience to the Roman Church. Neither does it appear anymore as the creation of a new church made up of pieces dispersed in diverse confessions. Visible unity presents itself as the reconciliation of sister-churches. Quite evidently, the community of faith between Orthodoxy and Catholicism with regard to the fundamental truths, the sacraments and their ministries explains the possibility of this reconciliation. But why shouldn't this concept of unity inscribe itself more and more in the heart of the relations between the Catholic Church and the churches of the Reform? Certainly, we can say that between Orthodoxy and Catholicism the only problem that remains is the infallibility and the universal and immediate jurisdiction of the pope. As regards the relations between Catholicism and Protestantism, many other difficulties present themselves.

However, the ecumenical dialogue has helped unity in faith to progress between Catholics and Protestants. The council is a striking sign of this. Indeed, much remains to be done; but we are committed to the road to unity. In this forward progress life is as important as theology. We must make unity at the same time as we think about it.

The future of Christianity requires the reconstitution of visible unity between the churches, and without it the evangelization of the world will be increasingly compromised. How can men believe in the gospel of love and peace if it is proclaimed competitively by churches that cannot manage to understand or accept each other in one same eucharistic communion? This scandal is no longer tolerable. But the history of the primitive church, as well as the contemporary world, teaches us that this unity is compatible with the diversity of local churches, particular theologies, diverse currents of spirituality and liturgies adapted to the cultural situations of men. Why can't there be tomorrow, in one same city, a community of the Roman Catholic type and another of the Lutheran type answering to diverse spiritual needs which correspond to different historical evolutions and different natures of men? Aren't there Catholic temperaments and Protestant temperaments which can subsist in unity and even enrich it by their diversity? The essential thing is that the local churches, or the diverse spiritual communities, be in intercommunion in one same fundamental faith, in the sharing of one Eucharist and in a mutually recognized ministry.

This means that visible unity in one same Eucharist will not be the final rewarding prize for an effort of total unification of the churches that are today separated. Soon, perhaps, in the march of the divided local or confessional churches towards their fundamental unity, a moment will come, a moment chosen by God, when they will be sufficiently near to each other to be able to give themselves to Christ, present in the Eucharist which they will take together, so that he himself may accomplish this unity in diversity by overturning the last obstacles which our theological limitations prevent us from surmounting.

Conclusion

The secularization of the world, far from compromising the future of Christianity, invites it to a salutary purification. Secularization obliges the church to a renewal of language to transmit, today and tomorrow, in a new and convincing way the eternal and immutable truth of the word of God. In order to accomplish this hermeneutical effort in a healthy and faithful manner, the church should renew itself in its life of prayer because it is only in contemplation of Christ, who is the Truth, that the truth of the gospel is able to be heard.

The church should also be ready to make all of the institutional simplifications which, in the upheavals of tomorrow, will enable it to remain faithful to its fundamental and necessary structure. This should be done without losing anything of what makes it the sign of God's presence in the world, the community of the baptized, witness to the gospel, united around Christ who is really present in the Eucharist and led by the Holy Spirit who distributes gifts and ministries as he wishes.

But the church can be faithful to its profound nature and keep its faith alive, its hope fervent, its charity ardent, only if it rediscovers soon in a spirit of sacrifice the fundamental unity of local and confessional churches, sister-churches, which will permit with the proper diversity of their riches their communion in the one meal of the Lord.

The future of Christianity is that the world should believe. It will not believe if the church remains divided much longer. The world can believe if love and peace radiate authentically from the refound unity of Christians. From the beginning Christ has prayed for this: "May they be one, so that the world may believe." Christianity's future depends on the answer to this prayer.